Biblical Hebrew
a homeschool primer

This student text and workbook is designed to be accompanied by **Biblical Hebrew: Annotations and Answers**, *a teacher's manual with answers, details, suggestions for use and supplemental resources, and an original audio CD of traditional Hebrew songs.*

Also available:

Biblical Hebrew: Show and Tell, *a DVD supplement to this primer, which offers stories from history and tradition with photos of places and wildlife in Israel, Biblical sites, art and artifacts; pronunciation of each lesson; and audiovisual flashcard review*

The Jonah Copybook, *an interlinear translation workbook, designed for use after this primer to develop fluency and give students a foothold in grammar, syntax, idiom, and translation*

Student Text and Workbook

Biblical Hebrew
a homeschool primer

Kim McKay

ALEF PRESS

ALEF PRESS

1036 Chestnut Hill Road
Cambridge, New York 12816
USA
www.alefpress.org

ISBN-13: 978-0-9881738-6-6

Printed in the United States of America

Acknowledgements

Kristen Niles and David Weeks are my gracious, godly, musical friends who perform the Hebrew songs for you.

Kristen homeschools her four daughters on a homestead with draft horses, chickens, turtles, and a dog. She studied music education at The King's College and has always loved to sing God's praises.

David Weeks is a farmer, musician, and songwriter whose generous good humor graces much more than this music. We have been delighted to see God's work in our lives through this project and pray that the thrill continues in you with your studies.

Thanks to the Niles and McKay kids, four of whom were baptized in the course of producing this book!

Thanks are due all the people through the ages who have cherished and preserved God's Word, written and kept alive this music, and established the religious and educational freedoms that we enjoy.

Neither this book, nor much else, would be possible without my husband's *chesed*, my mom's *chochmah*, and the Lord's *rachamim*.

Kim McKay

About the Author

The McKays' faith and family have been enriched mightily by learning Hebrew in their homeschool. Kim has written curricula, created exhibits, and led learning adventures for museums, educational farms, nature sanctuaries, and schools in the U.S. and U.K.

שִׂים שָׁלוֹם טוֹבָה וּבְרָכָה חַיִּים חֵן
וָחֶסֶד וְרַחֲמִים עָלֵינוּ וְעַל כָּל יִשְׂרָאֵל עַמֶּךָ

בָּרְכֵנוּ אָבִינוּ כֻּלָּנוּ כְּאֶחָד
בְּאוֹר פָּנֶיךָ כִּי בְאוֹר פָּנֶיךָ נָתַתָּ לָנוּ
אֲדֹנָי אֱלֹהֵינוּ
תּוֹרַת חַיִּים וְאַהֲבַת חֶסֶד וּצְדָקָה וּבְרָכָה
וְרַחֲמִים וְחַיִּים וְשָׁלוֹם

Table of Contents

Acknowledgements
About the Author

PART ONE: Alef-Bet Workbook

PART ONE

Alef-Bet Workbook

In the Hebrew language we hear God speak...thus study directed toward learning this language might rightly be called a kind of worship.

Martin Luther

Introduction

Learning Hebrew is sweet. To prove this to their little children, parents have, through the centuries, traditionally spread honey on their young scholar's slate on the first day of lessons. The child would happily lap it up. "Learning Hebrew," his parents would enthuse, "is even sweeter!"

Why honey? Psalm 19 says God's words are "sweeter also than honey and drippings of the honeycomb." And why so excited about learning the Hebrew alphabet? Because it was the first step to hearing God speak, to studying the words which the Creator Himself has given on life, the universe, and everything. What could be better?

this spot reserved for honey

Learning Hebrew remains a splendid way to grow in understanding of and love for God's Word. As the poet Haim Nachman Bialik once said, "Reading the Bible in translation is like kissing your new bride through a veil." Perhaps the best way to grow in insight and zeal for the Bible is to live what you learn there. My hope for this course is that your learning will bring joy and wisdom, the wisdom from above that is full of good deeds.

Lesson 1: Alphabet History

The world's oldest alphabet writing comes from Sinai and Canaan at the time of the Exodus. The letters are named for objects and resemble Egyptian signs already in use for those objects. For example,

Old Hebrew name for ox	Egyptian sign for ox	Early alphabet sign	Hebrew alphabet name for corresponding letter
alef			alef

Old Hebrew name for house	Egyptian sign for house	Early alphabet sign	Hebrew alphabet name for corresponding letter
bet			bet

The glory of an alphabet is that instead of having many signs to correspond with many objects, each sign represents a sound. We have thousands of things to talk about, but only about forty sounds we make. The alphabet lets us write about everything in the universe with a few symbols. This innovative simplicity made writing and reading much more practical for sharing information and easier to understand clearly.

Why did the alphabet get invented? The poet William Blake wrote that "God... in mysterious Sinai's awful cave/ To Man the wondrous art of writing gave." Historians usually credit the Canaanite merchants, not God. However it happened, the alphabet appeared just when and where it was needed to record the most important writing the world has ever known: God's Word.

Ever wondered what script God used to write the Ten Commandments in stone? It wouldn't have been exactly the letters you are about to learn. The Old Hebrew letters underwent some changes during Judah's Babylonian captivity. But the alphabet of Canaan and Sinai is recognizable in the Hebrew alphabet, and believe it or not, in the ABC's you learned as a tyke.

Greece picked up the alphabet from the Canaanites. *Alef, bet, gimel, dalet* became *alpha, beta, gamma, delta.* But there were no letters for vowel sounds until the Greeks got hold of the alphabet. (alphabet = alpha-beta = alef-bet: get it?) Before the Greeks, there wasn't any punctuation, either! The Romans adopted Greek gods and Greek letters. The letters you are reading right now come more or less straight from Rome and are known as the Latin letters. Have a look at the chart on the next page and Hebrew characters will not seem like such strangers when you meet them.

Letter name	Phoenician	Early Hebrew 10th C B.C.	Modern Hebrew	Early Greek	Classical Greek	Greek letter name	Latin
alef			א			alpha	A
bet			ב			beta	B
gimel			ג			gamma	C,G
dalet			ד			delta	D
hey			ה			epsilon	E
vav			ו			digamm	F,U,V,Y
zayin			ז			zeta	Z
chet			ח			eta	H
tet			ט			theta	
yud			י			iota	I
kaf			כ			kappa	K
lamed			ל			lambda	L
mem			מ			mu	M
nun			נ			nu	N
samech			ס			xi	X
ayin			ע			omicron	O
pey			פ			pi	P
tzadi			צ			san	
kuf			ק			qoppa	Q
resh			ר			rho	R
shin			ש			sigma	S
tav			ת			tau	T

Lesson 2: Alef

א is silent. A silent letter? Does this make sense? Alef is only a throaty little puff of breath sound. Though it hasn't much to say, alef keeps syllables from slurring together. We do not mark this effect with a letter in English, but you can feel it in your throat if you say aloud "an old." We don't say "a nold;" at the beginning of "old" is that throaty little puff of breath. Don't worry about adding any puffs into words, just treat alef as a real, but silent letter and it will happen naturally. Despite its silence, alef begins some very important words, for instance:

אַהֲבָה   (ah-ha-vah)   Love

אֱמֶת   (eh-met)   Truth

See the א there on the *right* of each word? Hebrew reads right to left.

Egyptian hieroglyphs were read according to the way the

signs were facing. If a bird symbol faced left, the reader knew to read left to right. Early Canaanite and Greek alphabet writing reversed direction on alternate lines. This is called "boustrophedon," or "as the ox plows" writing. The letters would face in the direction the words were going. Try writing some English boustrophedon. Write the first line normally, and then on the second line, go right to left with backwards letters.

→HELLO

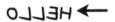

Eventually, Hebrew stuck with right to left, and Greek settled on left to right.

אֱמֶת (eh-met)   Truth

אָמֵן (ah-mane)   Amen

אֱמֶת looks and sounds a lot like "amen" because they come from the same root meaning firm and trustworthy. That's why we say "amen" at the end of a prayer: it means, "That's the truth and I affirm it!"

Amen has the distinction of being the world's most travelled word. It has entered straight into over one thousand languages. Perhaps everyone you will ever meet knows a little Hebrew.

Practice writing אָ.

←

X

Find and circle אָ in these Bible verses:

וְאָכַלְתָּ וְשָׂבָעְתָּ וּבֵרַכְתָּ אֶת־יְהֹוָה אֱלֹהֶיךָ עַל־הָאָרֶץ הַטֹּבָה אֲשֶׁר נָתַן־לָךְ׃

And you shall eat and be full, and you shall bless the LORD your God for the good land he has given you.   Deuteronomy 9:10

לֹא בְצִדְקָתְךָ וּבְיֹשֶׁר לְבָבְךָ אַתָּה בָא לָרֶשֶׁת אֶת־אַרְצָם כִּי בְּרִשְׁעַת הַגּוֹיִם הָאֵלֶּה יְהֹוָה אֱלֹהֶיךָ מוֹרִישָׁם מִפָּנֶיךָ וּלְמַעַן הָקִים אֶת־הַדָּבָר אֲשֶׁר נִשְׁבַּע יְהֹוָה לַאֲבֹתֶיךָ לְאַבְרָהָם לְיִצְחָק וּלְיַעֲקֹב

Not because of your righteousness or the uprightness of your heart are you going in to possess their land, but because of the wickedness of these nations the LORD your God is driving them out from before you, and that he may confirm the word that the LORD swore to your fathers, to Abraham, to Isaac, and to Jacob.   Deuteronomy 9:5

Now look back and underline the following alef word in each verse. It means "your God": אֱלֹהֶיךָ

Lesson 3: Bet

בּ and בּ are really one letter, but see the difference? That dot in the middle, called the "dagesh," changes the sound. Bet (**bate**) sounds like **b** as in **boy** with a dagesh; **v** as in **very** without. We can refer to bet without a dagesh as "vet" (**vate**).

You will meet two other letters that change sound with an inner point. Dagesh appears in the other letters without changing their pronunciation.

בּ was originally a picture of a house. The Hebrew word for house is בַּיִת (**bah-yeet**). But בַּיִת means more than four walls and roof. The בַּיִת of someone can also mean the people who live in the בַּיִת, as in Genesis 18:19 and Luke 10:5:

For I have chosen him, that he may command his children and his **household** after him to keep the way of the LORD by doing righteousness and justice, so that the LORD may bring to Abraham what he has promised him. Genesis 18:19

Whatever **house** you enter, first say, "Peace be to this **house!**" Luke 10:5

בַּיִת can also mean a dynasty, as in this passage:

And to the **house** of the king of Judah say, "Hear the word of the LORD, O **House** of David! Jeremiah 21:11-12a

The "beth" in Bethlehem and all the other Beth-so-and-so place names in the Bible is a form of בַּיִת. These place names all mean the house of something: the home of the rock, bread, the sun, lions, apples, fishing.

בַּיִת is also used to mean a temple because that is essentially what a temple is: a home for a god.

Practice writing בּ and בּ . Pronounce each letter aloud as you
write it.

בּ

בּ

Find and circle בּ and בּ in this Bible verse. Look out! There is a
very similar Hebrew letter. Do not circle כּ and כ.

וַעֲשֵׂה־לִי מַטְעַמִּים כַּאֲשֶׁר אָהַבְתִּי וְהָבִיאָה לִי וְאֹכֵלָה בַּעֲבוּר
תְּבָרֶכְךָ נַפְשִׁי בְּטֶרֶם אָמוּת

and prepare for me delicious food, such as I love, and bring it to me so that I may eat, that my soul
may bless you before I die.   Genesis 27:4

Find and circle the letters in each line that are the same as the first.

ב   פסבמייבכרטכשקלבנכזגאיתטמןפבהבט

ב   צכנאבלפתטיקבזדכליעכברתפסמנגבהכ

א   שאפבישנליופשאגהאזכלמאטעעחןשאצ

Lesson 4: Gimel

ג makes the sound of **g** as in **goat**.

ג was once a picture of a camel, which in Hebrew is called a *gamal*. Gamal...gimel...camel...see the connection?

גָּדוֹל (gah-dole) is a *big* word in Hebrew. It means "big" or "great." In the Bible you will find, for example, גָּדוֹל whales, גָּדוֹל strength, גָּדוֹל noise, a גָּדוֹל golden crown, גָּדוֹל wickedness, and גָּדוֹל faithfulness and love. *Great* stuff.

Practice writing ג. Pronounce each letter aloud as you write it.

ג

Find and circle the gimels in this Bible verse. ג = ג

וְעִבְרִים עָבְרוּ אֶת־הַיַּרְדֵּן אֶרֶץ גָּד וְגִלְעָד וְשָׁאוּל עוֹדֶנּוּ בַגִּלְגָּל וְכָל־
הָעָם חָרְדוּ אַחֲרָיו

...and some Hebrews crossed the fords of the Jordan to the land of Gad and Gilead. Saul was still at Gilgal, and all the people followed him trembling.   1 Samuel 13:7

Looking at the translation, can you explain why there are plenty of gimels in this verse?
Look at the verse again and underline alef and bet. ב counts, too.

Find and circle the letters in each line that are the same as the first.

הכנדבתרפזלושבחקכמירסמזבאגומאכת   ב

רשגאלבפדאוךצלאיחצנקאכלפאהתתצצש   א

הנדגפאבגלזרענתוגבנליופאכהגשנאבטג   ג

Lesson 5: Vowel Points

Remember that the Greeks first used letters to represent vowel sounds? The Hebrew alphabet had no vowels. Reading was a bit like this: "Rdng ws bt lk ths." Readers discerned the meaning and pronunciation from their knowledge of the spoken language and context. This is still how fluent Hebrew speakers read and write. But a system of vowel indications has been worked out for accuracy and beginners. These vowel points are the dots and dashes you see floating around Hebrew letters.

A sentence with vowel points:

וַיַּעֲלוּ מִמִּצְרָיִם וַיָּבֹאוּ אֶרֶץ כְּנַעַן אֶל־יַעֲקֹב אֲבִיהֶם

The same sentence without vowel points:

ויעלו ממצרים ויבאו ארץ כנען אל־יעקב אביהם

All the Hebrew letters, even silent ones, are consonants. Vowels are written below or beside consonants, one vowel per consonant. Pronounce the letter, then its vowel. When a vowel appears with a silent consonant, pronounce the vowel only.

Let's learn two of the Hebrew vowels and use them with consonants you know.

אָ = אַ = **ah** as in **mama**

בָּ = בַּ = **bah**

בָ = בַ = **vah**

גָ = גַ = **gah**

Practice writing letters with vowels. Copy these syllables onto the line below them.

גַ גָ בַ בָ בַּ אַ אָ בָּ

Find and circle the vowel points that you have met in this verse.

בְּרֵאשִׁית בָּרָא אֱלֹהִים אֵת הַשָּׁמַיִם וְאֵת הָאָרֶץ

In the beginning, God created the heavens and the earth.   Genesis 1:1

Read Hebrew! Pronounce each syllable aloud.

בֶּ בַ בְ גַ אָ גָ בָ גְ אַ בֶּ ←

גְ אַ בְ בָ גְ בֶ בֶּ גְ אַ אָ ←

אָ גְ בַ בָ גָ אַ גְ בָ אָ בֶּ ←

Lesson 6: Dalet

ד sounds like **d** as in **day**.

דָּבָר (**dah-var**) means *both* "word" and "thing." The Bible certainly considers words to be real, substantial, and powerful. Think of how all Creation came to be. God did not sculpt it, mix it, draw it, write plans, or even just imagine it: He spoke words.

God considers human speech to be weighty, too. There are commandments requiring testimony to be given in court, rebukes to be delivered, promises to be kept, and stories to be told. There are commandments forbidding slander, gossip, defamation, and curses on rulers. Proverbs 18:21 says, "Death and life are in the power of the tongue."

Scripture even calls God's words alive and life-giving. Words, so easily discounted in our culture, are not only as substantive as things, but some are much more so:

> Heaven and earth will pass away, but my words will not pass away.   Luke 21:33

Practice writing **ד**. Pronounce the letter aloud as you write.

Find and circle the letters in each line that are the same as the first.
Be careful for **ד** look-a-likes:

ד ﬡ ך ן ר ז ו

ד   ברא‌דחנכזגרלד‌ססקיפרהד‌צזמנזחרהגט

ג   פבוזאנהגפרך‌מגיחגורעצנפא‌אזליר‌עקנב

ד   ך‌לתצכ‌דערסזהכנ‌תד‌אשויפטר‌הגדללד‌מזי

א   צדשסעיפגבצצאוקאליהנארצסמהאכזפדו

Find and circle 7 in these verses. ד = ד

וַיְעַנְּךָ וַיַּרְעִבֶךָ וַיַּאֲכִלְךָ אֶת־הַמָּן אֲשֶׁר לֹא־יָדַעְתָּ וְלֹא יָדְעוּן אֲבֹתֶיךָ
לְמַעַן הוֹדִיעֲךָ כִּי לֹא עַל־הַלֶּחֶם לְבַדּוֹ יִחְיֶה הָאָדָם כִּי עַל־כָּל־מוֹצָא
פִי־יְהוָה יִחְיֶה הָאָדָם

And he humbled you and let you hunger and fed you with manna, which you did not know, that he might make you know that man does not live by bread alone, but man lives by every word that comes from the mouth of the LORD.   Deuteronomy 8:3

דָּבָר שָׁלַח אֲדֹנָי בְּיַעֲקֹב וְנָפַל בְּיִשְׂרָאֵל

The Lord has sent a word against Jacob, and it will fall on Israel.   Isaiah 9:8 (7)

In the verse above, which Hebrew word means "word"? Did you wonder what that (7) in the Scripture reference means? In an English Bible, this verse is labeled Isaiah 9:8, but in a Hebrew Bible, it appears as Isaiah 9:7. Chapter and verse numbers are not inspired and vary slightly in a few places.

Read these syllables aloud: ←

דַ אָ בְ גְ דַ דְ אַ דָ בְ גָ בַ בַ

אַ דַ בְ גַ דְ אָ בְ גָ בְ בַ

Those last syllables started with a consonant and had a vowel. Some Hebrew syllables start with a consonant, have a vowel, and then one more consonant on the end. Read these aloud:

בַּד אַב אָג בֵּב בָּ דַד גָב בַּ בֵּ אָא

דָב גַד בָּא אָד דָב בַּ דַב בֵּ דָג גָא

בֵּ בָּג אַב דָא בָ בָּא אָב בֵּ בָּ

Congratulations, you just read a real Hebrew word! אָב means "father."

Lesson 7: Hey

ה sounds like **h** as in **hen**. הָ and הַ sound like **hah**.

Attached to a Hebrew word as a prefix, הָ or הַ means "the."

$$\text{הַדָּבָר} \quad = \quad \text{דָּבָר} \quad + \quad \text{הַ} \leftarrow$$

$$\text{the word} \quad = \quad \text{word} \quad + \quad \text{the} \leftarrow$$

"The" never stands alone in Hebrew. Neither do possessive pronouns like "his" and "your." Possessive pronouns get attached to words as suffixes. Many prepositions are prefixes. The basic idea in Hebrew is that root words made of three consonants hold steady while vowels change and additions are made to give shades of meaning.

Practice writing ה:

ה

Find and circle ה in this Bible verse:

וַיְהִי בַּיּוֹם הַשְּׁמִינִי קָרָא מֹשֶׁה לְאַהֲרֹן וּלְבָנָיו וּלְזִקְנֵי יִשְׂרָאֵל

On the eighth day Moses called Aaron and his sons and the elders of Israel,   Leviticus 9:1

Which ה in the verse above means "the"?

At the end of a word, ה is silent if it does not have a vowel.

בָּה = בָּ

Look again at the Bible verse above. Find the silent ה.

How many ways can you spell the sound **bah** with Hebrew letters?
Write them below. See if you can come up with six different ways.

בָּ   בָ

Read aloud:

←

גָ הַג הָג דָב דַה בָ אַה גָה בַג ה הָ

בַ אַה אַג הַב גָה הַד גָד הַד בָה בָד

אַ גַב בָא הַב גָה גָא דָב בַג דָה

Spell the English words below with Hebrew letters.

English word	spell it with Hebrew
hog	
hob	
god	
bog	
bob	

Lesson 8: Vav

וֹ sounds like **v** as in **very**, same as בֿ.

וֹ , with a vowel and attached as a prefix, means "and." Like "the," "and" does not stand alone as a Hebrew word.

$$\text{וְהַמֶּלֶךְ} = \text{מֶלֶךְ} + \text{הַ} + \text{וְ} \leftarrow$$
and the king   king   the   and

When וֹ is a prefix of a verb, it can change the tense, too:

and will go = went + וַ ←

and kept = will keep + וַ ←

Did you ever notice that so many Bible sentences begin with "and"? As in, "And the LORD spoke to Moses, saying..." or as in, "And God said, 'Let there be light.' And it was so." Beginning many sentences with "and" is bad form in English. When I was a kid, I even wondered why God hadn't arranged for proper grammar on such an important project.

In reality, many Hebrew sentences begin with verbs and many Hebrew verbs have a ו prefix to change the tense. It is not at all bad form in Hebrew to begin sentences with ו.

ו as a prefix can also mean "now," "but," "then," or "so." The translator chooses. You can see how translation can tweak interpretation, and vice versa.

While we are on, "And the LORD spoke to Moses, saying...," did that "saying" ever seem awkward to you? It is there in the Hebrew because quotation marks are not! The Greeks introduced punctuation, remember. Hebrew throws in "saying" so that the reader will know that a direct quote follows.

If you have grown up thinking that the Old Testament sounded a bit clunky and cumbersome, you are going to love studying Hebrew. Hebrew is pithy, concise, and vigorous. Getting past translation clumsiness will bring the Bible alive!

ו is a consonant, but ו with dots gives us new vowel sounds:

v as in **very** = ו

oo (with no **v** sound) = וּ

oh (with no **v** sound) = וֹ

So,

וָ = vah   בוּ = boo   גוֹ = go

Occasionally, vav has an inner point *and* a vowel. In that case, both the **v** sound and vowel are pronounced.

vah = וַ   **voh** = וֹ

Find and circle ו וֹ וּ in these Bible verses:

זֹאת עֲבֹדַת מִשְׁפְּחֹת בְּנֵי מְרָרִי לְכָל־עֲבֹדָתָם בְּאֹהֶל מוֹעֵד בְּיַד
אִיתָמָר בֶּן־אַהֲרֹן הַכֹּהֵן: וַיִּפְקֹד מֹשֶׁה וְאַהֲרֹן וּנְשִׂיאֵי הָעֵדָה אֶת־
בְּנֵי הַקְּהָתִי לְמִשְׁפְּחֹתָם וּלְבֵית אֲבֹתָם:

This is the service of the clans of the sons of Merari, the whole of their service in the tent of
meeting, under the direction of Ithamar the son of Aaron the priest. And Moses and Aaron and the
chiefs of the congregation listed the sons of the Kohathites, by their clans and their fathers' houses
Numbers 4:33-34

Translation from Hebrew is often wordy, but Hebrew is not.
Compare the number of words it took to say the same thing in the
verses above in Hebrew versus English.

Practice writing. Pronounce each letter aloud as you write:

←

ךְ

וֹ

ךֶ

Read aloud:

הוּ   דוּ   וַב   בָּ   וַד   גוֹ   דוּ   בּוֹ   וַ   וְ

הוּ   הוֹג   הָג   דָב   וַב   בּוּ   הָא   הוּ   בוּ

הוֹד   דוֹב   גוּד   וֹו   וָד   וַו   גוֹד   הוֹג

Spell the sounds of these English words with Hebrew letters:

English word	spell it with Hebrew	English word	spell it with Hebrew
go		dude	
do		hove	
hoe		bode	
ha-ha		goad	
dog		who	
vogue		goo	

Match the Hebrew words and their meanings:

אַהֲבָה   truth

דָּבָר   big

וְ   word/thing

בַּיִת   love

אֱמֶת   the

הַ   and

גָּדוֹל   house

You are learning the Hebrew letters in alphabetical order, and it will be useful to remember that sequence. Sing the Alef-Bet Song regularly to make memorization a snap.

Lesson 9: Zayin

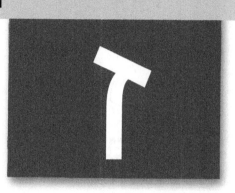

זָ (**zy-yeen**) sounds like **z** as in **zoo**.

זֶרַע (**zeh-rah**) means "seed." God promised that Abraham's זֶרַע would be given the land of Canaan, that Abraham's זֶרַע would be innumerable as the dust and the stars, and that in Abraham's זֶרַע all nations of earth would be blessed. Your Bible might use the word "offspring." In Hebrew, it is זֶרַע

In Hebrew, as in English, "seed" can be a singular or collective noun: "one *seed*" or "a bag of *seed*." The Apostle Paul uses this grammatical point in Galatians 3:16 and 3:29:

> Now the promises were made to Abraham and to his [seed]. It does not say, "And to [seeds]," referring to many, but referring to one, "And to your [seed]," who is

Christ... And if you are Christ's, then you are Abraham's [seed], heirs according to promise.

Jesus is the singular *seed* of Abraham in whom God's promises are ultimately fulfilled, blessing all the nations, who are the bag of *seed*. A גָּדוֹל bag of זֶרַע !

Practice writing ז:

ז

Find and circle ז in this passage:

וְשַׂמְתִּי אֶת־זַרְעֲךָ כַּעֲפַר הָאָרֶץ אֲשֶׁר אִם־יוּכַל אִישׁ לִמְנוֹת אֶת־עֲפַר
הָאָרֶץ גַּם־זַרְעֲךָ יִמָּנֶה:

I will make your offspring as the dust of the earth, so that if one can count the dust of the earth, your offspring also can be counted.   Genesis 13:16

Look again and find "and." "The" appears twice; see it?

Copy and pronounce these syllables:

אַז   זוּב   בּוֹז   הַז   זָג

_____

זָא   זוּ   הוּז   גּוֹה   הוֹב

_____

Draw a picture or symbol to represent each word below:

בֵּית	אַהֲבָה
גָּדוֹל	זֶרַע

Lesson 10: CHet

ח

ח represents a sound that English got from German but gave up centuries ago in an attempt to be French. We will write this sound as **CH**, but you may see it in Hebrew transliterations as "ch," "ẖ," "ḥ," "kh," or "H." **CH** is not the "ch" in "church," but the soft, throaty "ch" in "Bach" or "loch."

You see, German, English, and Scots have common roots which included the **CH** sound, but William the Conqueror's success at Hastings in 1066 made French the *chic* language of England. And they say that **"sheek,"** not **"CHeek."** (Just try pronouncing **CHeek**, and you will see why!) So the English dropped **CH** and started fishing in lakes, while the Scots, who were not so overrun with Normans, kept on fishing in lo**CH**s.

Despite what the French may think, ח makes a lovely sound and ח has the honor of beginning some of the most wonderful words in the Bible:

grace	(**CH**ane)	חֵן
wisdom	(**CH**o**CH**-mah)	חָכְמָה
life	(**CH**ai-yeem)	חַיִּים
steadfast love	(**CH**ess-ed)	חֶסֶד

As Job said (paraphrasing here), "You gotta take the bad with the good." Perhaps ח agrees. ח also begins חֲטָא (**CH**ate), or "sin," which means "missing the mark," as in archery. God's Word is the target at which we aim.

Practice writing ח. Notice how it differs from ה.

חָ

Find and circle the letters in each line that are the same as the first.
Look-alike alert:

ח ≠ ה ת

ה   גחפעתכהבלוהוחמזצתשאקהלפיברךחנהי

ת   צהופירסחכתצזץאטמסלדאתרעשיהבחות

Write the English word that these nonsense Hebrew syllables sound like:

English homophone	Hebrew syllable	English homophone	Hebrew syllable
	בָּג		זוּ
	דוֹז		הוּז
	גָז		בַח
	אוֹז		ווֹג

Match the Hebrew words and their meanings:

חֶסֶד   grace

חָכְמָה   sin

הֵן   life

חֵטְא   steadfast love

דָּבָר   wisdom

חַיִּים   word/thing

Read aloud:

חוּ חוֹ חָ חַ הֵ הָ הוּ הוֹ הֵח הַח זָא

זַח בּוֹח הוּו אָח בּו וַד דוּג בָּא דַ

הוּו דוּג אַב זוּ בּוֹד בּוֹה דַח אוּד

חוֹד חַד בָּז זוּז דוֹח אוּו הוֹב אַה

בּוֹא זַח דוֹה בָּח וָה אַג אוֹז אוּד

דַה אַז גָו גוּ זוֹח חוֹה בּוּא חָג

חָג (in the star) is a real Hebrew word meaning "festival." You can give holiday greetings by saying, " חַג שָׂמֵחַ (**CH**ahg sah-may-a**CH**)." חָג comes from a root word meaning to go round in a circle, because round dancing was such a notable component of celebrations!

Lesson 11: Tet

ט sounds like **t** as in **tart**.

Look at this! טוֹב You can already read this word!

טוֹב means "good." It works as an adjective ("good"), as a noun ("goodness"), and as an adverb ("well"). טוֹב is what God had to say about His works of creation: "And God saw that it was טוֹב."

Find and underline טוֹב in this Bible verse:

יָדַעְתִּי כִּי אֵין טוֹב בָּם כִּי אִם־לִשְׂמוֹחַ וְלַעֲשׂוֹת טוֹב בְּחַיָּיו

I perceived that there is nothing better for them than to be joyful and to do good as long as they live... Ecclesiastes 3:12

Did you find them both? Look again and find "and."   Now find ח.

Practice writing ט:

Read aloud:

חַ גַז חַ טַא ווֹג חַט טָב טַב טוּ טוֹ

Try two syllables:

חַטוֹ טוֹדָא הָזוּ זוּךְ טַ הוֹדָה בָּ

גְדוֹה טָב וְדוֹא הוֹדוּ בְּבוֹ בַּ בוֹדוּ

טַדוֹה זוֹוַא בוֹדָה חַדוּ בָּטָה דוּגוֹ

Spell these English words with Hebrew letters, then read your writing aloud:

English word	spell it with Hebrew	English word	spell it with Hebrew
go		dot	
got		goat	
hose		hot	
Bach		boat	
boot		hoot	
two		toga	

Match the Hebrew words and their meanings:

good   חָכְמָה

sin   וְ־

house   אֶמֶת

seed   בַּיִת

truth   הַ־

the   חֵטְא

wisdom   זֶרַע

and   טוֹב

Lesson 12: Yud

Please do not think that learning Hebrew is useful "only for Old Testament studies." The New Testament authors were all Hebrew speakers. Hebrew thought and language underlie the whole Bible. Knowing Hebrew can illuminate passages in Greek. Let's look at one simple example.

Did you ever wonder what those unshakable "jots" and "tittles" in Matthew 5:18 are? Please meet the jot: ׳. He is not really a "jot." He is a yud (**yude**).

He says **y** as in **yes**. There isn't a **j** as in **jot** sound in Hebrew at all. Or in Greek. Or in Classical Latin. But "j" got used to transliterate ׳ in English Bibles. All the Bible names you know that start with J never sounded like that in Hebrew. Sometimes they are not even close. יֵשׁוּעַ (Yeshua) has become known to us as "Jesus." Sometimes י was transliterated as an "i," as in Israel. Israel in Hebrew is יִשְׂרָאֵל (**Yeess-rah-ale**).

When you know Hebrew, Jesus' name is not just a collection of sounds. Every time you say יֵשׁוּעַ, you hear the Hebrew word for "salvation." This was God's intention:

> She will bear a son, and you shall call his name יֵשׁוּעַ, for he will save his people from their sins.
> Matthew 1:21

Practice writing י :

ך

Find and circle the words "Israel," "good," and "house" in this Bible verse:

וַיְדַבֵּר גַּם־אַבְנֵר בְּאָזְנֵי בִנְיָמִין וַיֵּלֶךְ גַּם־אַבְנֵר לְדַבֵּר בְּאָזְנֵי דָוִד בְּחֶבְרוֹן אֵת כָּל־אֲשֶׁר־טוֹב בְּעֵינֵי יִשְׂרָאֵל וּבְעֵינֵי כָּל־בֵּית בִּנְיָמִן

Abner also spoke to Benjamin. And then Abner went to tell David at Hebron all that Israel and the whole house of Benjamin thought good to do.   2 Samuel 3:19

Read aloud:

יָד יַג יוֹ יַח יוֹז יוֹב דוּבָ גוֹטוּ יוֹב

וַט יַהָא זוּ טוֹב דַבוּ יָדוּ יַג דוּה

גוֹא יוּ דַיָא אוֹזַה יָד יוּד יוֹט

אוֹדוּא בוּ ווֹדַה זוּז חַד טַח בוּ

יוּזָא בָּבוּ

How many ways can you spell the sound **yah** with Hebrew letters?
Write six different ways below:

׳ sounds like "y" and acts a bit like it, too. "Y" is a consonant in "yes," but can join a vowel to represent a vowel sound, as in "ay-yi-yi" or "joy." ׳ does this, too.

When the vowel sound "ah" is followed directly by yud, the sound changes to "**aye**."

"buy" = בַּי   "dye" = דָי

"eye" = אַי   "guy" = גַי

Read aloud:

בַּי אָי זַי דַיא בּוֹדִי זָידוֹ דִי חַי

בָּדִי בּוֹזַיא הָיד אַיד טוֹדִי בָיו בּוּ

When וֹ is followed by ׳, they combine to sound like "**oy**" (much as do the "o" and "y" in "boy").

"boy" = בּוֹי   "toy" = טוֹי

Read aloud:

בּוֹי גּוֹי הוֹי זוֹי אַגּוֹי דוֹי גּוֹיד

אוֹי הַדוֹי אוֹבּוֹי

Spell these English words with Hebrew letters, then read your writing aloud:

English word	spell it with Hebrew	English word	spell it with Hebrew
boy		zoo	
dough		bow-tie	
bye		toy	
toe		hi	
yacht		yo-yo	

Lesson 13: Hebrew Numerals

You have seen Roman numerals. They look like letters. They *are* letters! The letters represent the numbers as well as spoken sounds. Greek and Hebrew letters were used this way, too. The numbers have their own names, but they are represented in writing by the letters, in order, so:

6 = ו   1 = א
7 = ז   2 = ב
8 = ח   3 = ג
9 = ט   4 = ד
10 = י   5 = ה

You may have seen in paintings or sculpture the Ten Commandments represented by Hebrew letters. Some modern Hebrew Bibles use the Hebrew letters for chapter and verse notations. Things get trickier after ten. The letters start counting by tens and hundreds. See Appendix B for details.

You realize this means you can work sudoku puzzles with Hebrew letters, don't you? Now is your chance. To solve these puzzles, every number from 1-9 (that is, alef to tet) must be placed in each of the nine horizontal rows, each of the nine vertical columns, and in each of the nine boxes.

ט					ח	ז		ב
	ד		א	ג			ח	
ח		ו	ט			ה		
ד			ז		ה	ג	ט	
	ה						ב	
	ט	ח	ד		ו			ז
		ד			א	ט		ה
	ח			ו	ד		ג	
א		ה	ב					ח

א		ו		ג			ב	ד
ד				ח	א			
		ט	ו			ג		ה
	ז		ד		ג	ב		
ב	ד						ט	ג
		ה	ט		ב		ד	
ו		ז			ה	ד		
			ב	ד				ט
ח	ט			ו		ה		ב

What number do you think this **יד** is? It is 10 plus 4: 14.
Complete these equations:

$$\text{יג} - \text{ז} = 6$$

$$\text{ג} + \text{ד} = 7$$

$$\text{ו} + \text{א} + \text{ה} = 12$$

$$\text{ב} + \text{ח} = 10$$

Lesson 14: Kaf

כ is like בּ: it can appear without the dagesh (dot in the middle) and make a different sound while still being the same letter. כּ makes the sound of **k** as in **kite**. כ sounds just the same as ח: it has the lovely soft **CH** sound in **loch** and **Bach**.

Write kaf and **CH**af below. Pronounce them aloud as you write:

There is one more **CH**af yet! כ has a different shape when written as the last consonant in a word. This is a bit like the difference between uppercase and lowercase letters in English: same letter, same sound, different shape. The good news is that only five Hebrew letters have a special final-letter form. These final-letter forms are called by their usual name plus the word "sofit" (**sew-feet**). So, please meet the **CH**af Sofit: ך. It sounds just like כ and ח.

Write and pronounce ך. Notice that it must continue below the line to not be ד.

ך usually appears with two dots in it: ךְ. This does not change the sound. You will often find **CH**af Sofit with the vowel *X*ָ, which is written inside, too: ךָ

Here is a kaf word you can read for yourself: כָּבוֹד. It means "honor." Its root meaning is "heaviness." "To honor" in Hebrew means "to give weight to," to recognize proper importance and authority. Which of the Ten Commandments begins with a form of כָּבוֹד ? ⁴ Which number commandment is that (in Hebrew letters, rather than Arabic numerals, of course!)? Dalet

---

Find and circle כ כ ך in this Bible verse:

וַיֹּאמֶר הִנֵּה אָנֹכִי כֹּרֵת בְּרִית נֶגֶד כָּל־עַמְּךָ אֶעֱשֶׂה נִפְלָאֹת אֲשֶׁר לֹא־
נִבְרְאוּ בְכָל־הָאָרֶץ וּבְכָל־הַגּוֹיִם וְרָאָה כָל־הָעָם אֲשֶׁר־אַתָּה בְקִרְבּוֹ
אֶת־מַעֲשֵׂה יְהוָה כִּי־נוֹרָא הוּא אֲשֶׁר אֲנִי עֹשֶׂה עִמָּךְ

And he said, "Behold, I am making a covenant. Before all your people I will do marvels, such as have not been created in all the earth or in any nation. And all the people among whom you are shall see the work of the LORD, for it is an awesome thing that I will do with you." Exodus 34:10

Find "and honor" in the verse below:

וַיָּמָת בְּשֵׂיבָה טוֹבָה שְׂבַע יָמִים עֹשֶׁר וְכָבוֹד וַיִּמְלֹךְ שְׁלֹמֹה בְנוֹ
תַּחְתָּיו

Then he died at a good age, full of days, riches, and honor. And Solomon his son reigned in his place.   1 Chronicles 29:28

Read aloud:

דְּבוֹי כּוֹי כּוֹדִי כַּבְ כְ כּוּ כּוֹ כַ כְּ

וָךְ בּוֹ טוֹי גַז דוֹךְ בּוֹךְ כּוֹה אַךְ

גוֹז בָּךְ חוֹכָא טוֹה אוֹךְ בּוֹדַךְ כּוֹב

כּוּכוֹ כָּדוֹ כָ טוֹךְ יָד טוֹךְ אָזִי כָּבוֹד

הָוָה בּוֹי הָכָא יַךְ בַּכְּט כּוֹזָה דַ

גוּ דוֹכַה הוֹוַה בּוֹאַד טָכָא כּוּ זוֹידָה

חַזִי כּוֹדָא בּוֹוךְ דַי כּוֹה טַכַה כָז

Lesson 15: A New Vowel

One dot below a letter represents **ee** as in **sheep**. ׳ often follows this vowel, but does not change the sound.

Read aloud:

גֶט כַּב כַּח הֵיב בִּי יוֹב יְד הֵד

בְּכַה טַא דְוִי כִּי כּוֹד גְדַה זְכַה יָד

טִיז ווֹט דָג הֵט דִיךְ כַּח אֵזוֹ בְט

בּוִי טַג דְוו כּוֹט וִיז הְבוּ כִּי הוִי

דַ וֹד כּוֹב כִּיט גְזָא כְּב כַּו דוּ

חַטָ טִיו גוֹי דַי הִי בּט חָג אָדוֹה

Spell the sounds of these English words with Hebrew letters:

English word	spell it with Hebrew	English word	spell it with Hebrew
tea		use	
beet		bead	
kite		void	
ooze		coy	
heat		key	
bite		boys	
Bach		bees	
cod		dye	

Match the Hebrew words and their translations:

honor	טוֹב
Israel	חֶסֶד
grace	יֵשׁוּעַ
good	חַיִּים
life	כָּבוֹד
steadfast love	יִשְׂרָאֵל
Jesus	הֵן

Lesson 16: Lamed

ל

ל sounds like **l** as in **land**.

לֶחֶם (le-CHem) means "food" or "bread." That shows you how important grains were in the ancient Middle Eastern diet. Yeshua (did you hear "salvation"?) taught us to pray, "Give us this day our daily לֶחֶם ." You will understand the whole Bible better if you study Israeli geography and agriculture. Summers are hot and dry, but winter is warm, with rains, so crops (to make לֶחֶם) grow during the winter to be harvested in spring. Passover is right at the barley harvest. Shavuot, aka Pentecost, aka The Feast of Weeks, coincides with the wheat harvest.

לֹא (**low**) means "no," or "do not." כֵּן (**cane**) is "yes." Try using לֹא and כֵּן with your family this week.

Practice writing lamed:

ל

Find לֹא in these verses from the Ten Commandments:

לֹא תִרְצָח׃   לֹא תִנְאָף׃   לֹא תִגְנֹב׃   לֹא־תַעֲנֶה בְרֵעֲךָ עֵד
שָׁקֶר׃

You shall not murder. You shall not commit adultery. You shall not steal. You shall not bear false witness against your neighbor.   Exodus 20:13-16

Read aloud:

לֵב   לַח   לֵוִי   גּוֹלִי   בָּל   לוּ   אֶל   טָל

חָא   גּוֹד   טוֹלוּ   אַד   לוּב   חַל   הֵיל

טַט   כֹּל   לוּךְ   הֵיל   כּוּל   כַּדּוּ   לָא

בּוֹ   דַּל   לוּז   כּוּ   בּוֹ   זוֹל   בּוֹט   בָּדוֹא

חֵל   כַּט   לִבִּי   אַדָּא   וִיל   וְיד   לִיד   הֵלוּ

גָּדוֹל   בַּל   כּוֹד   לֵוִי   הַיְד   גּוֹי   אִיל

In each blank, write the number of the Hebrew word that best completes the sentence:

ד. יִשְׂרָאֵל   א. אַהֲבָה

ה. הָ־   ב. זֶרַע

ו. גָּדוֹל   ג. חֵטְא

1. Jonah was swallowed by a _____ fish.

2. The LORD had told him to leave _____ and go to Nineveh.

3. Jonah had no great _____ for the Assyrians.

4. They were evil. They knew all about _____.

5. Jonah did not plant a _____, but nevertheless a plant grew up over him and gave him shade.

6. _____ plant withered when attacked by a worm. Jonah withered in the heat without shade.

אֵ = אֵי = **ay** as in **way**.

אֶ = אֶי = **e** as in **egg**.

Read aloud:

אֶל כֶט כֶּט חֶד אֶד וֶט טֶל בֶּל בֵּל בֵּי בֵּ

טֶך וֵי חֵי כֶּד לֵיב זֶד בֵּיז בֵּי בֵּ

חוּ דֶטָה לַדוּ דּוֹבֵי לֶך לֵב בֵּל אֶט

Spell the sounds of these English words with Hebrew letters:

English word	spell it with Hebrew	English word	spell it with Hebrew
Kate		kale	
light		yell	
teal		bed	
yet		cot	
boil		loot	
keel		tool	
date		gaze	
aisle		tail	
bait		zeal	
let		days	
Yale		easy	
cave		lazy	

Lesson 18: Mem

מ was once a picture of a wave. מ represents the sound of **m** as in **mom**.

Here is a מ word that you can already read: מֶלֶךְ מֶלֶךְ means "king." Translate: דָּוִד הַמֶּלֶךְ

מ also begins מְאֹד (**meh-ode**), which means "very." As God created the world, He saw that it was טוֹב. On Friday afternoon, after making man and woman in His image, He declared the whole wonderful world טוֹב מְאֹד.

Please note that mem has a sofit form: ם. The sofits may have helped readers distinguish words in the days when writingwasmorelikethisbecausethereerewerenospacesbetweenwords.

Practice writing מ and ם. Pronounce them as you write:

מ

ם

Find מ and ם in Scripture:

וַיִּסְעוּ מֵאֵילִם וַיָּבֹאוּ כָּל־עֲדַת בְּנֵי־יִשְׂרָאֵל אֶל מִדְבַּר־סִין אֲשֶׁר בֵּין־
אֵילִם וּבֵין סִינָי בַּחֲמִשָּׁה עָשָׂר יוֹם לַחֹדֶשׁ הַשֵּׁנִי לְצֵאתָם מֵאֶרֶץ
מִצְרָיִם

They set out from Elim, and all the congregation of the people of Israel came to the wilderness of Sin, which is between Elim and Sinai, on the fifteenth day of the second month after they had departed from the land of Egypt.   Exodus 16:1

Fill in the correct form of mem in these real Hebrew words:

שֶׁה ____   ____רִי ____   צְוָה ____

Moses   Miriam   commandment

Fill in the correct form of mem in these real Hebrew words:

מִי דְּבָּר___ ___ִי___
‎
who   desert   water

Circle the one in each line that rhymes with the first:

טוֹדָא   זָדוֹל הוֹדָה גוֹאֵל מוֹדִים

בָּבִים   דַוְם בַּלוֹם בַּזֶל דֶּבֶד

כָּבוֹד   מֶלֶךְ מָבוֹד דוֹטֵא כַּבֵל

Read aloud:

מוּ בָּם בֵּם לֶם מוֹדָה מַיִם לֵב מִי

מְדוֹה דֶם דוּל כֶם לִיבוּ טֵל כַּם

בוִי אֵם טִי מֶט טַם דוֹבוּ זֶךְ דִיל

Lesson 19: Nun

נ (**noon**) sounds like **n** as in **nut** and has a sofit form: ן.

נָבִיא means "prophet," one who is chosen to convey messages from God. Translate: מִיכָה הַנָּבִיא

The Hebrew Scriptures are sometimes called the "Tanach," which is an acronym for the Torah, Prophets, and Writings. Torah is the Pentateuch, Moses' books. Writings are books like Psalms, Proverbs, Job, and Ecclesiastes. The Prophets are the נְבִיאִים (plural of נָבִיא), and refer to the books of the prophets such as Hosea, Isaiah, and Micah. Jesus referred to this division system when he said, "...everything written about me in the Law of Moses and the Prophets and the Psalms must be fulfilled." (Luke 24:44)

Practice writing ב and ן. ן is distinguished from ו by continuing below the baseline. Nun sofit is distinguished from ך by having a shorter top crosspiece that does not extend to the right. Pronounce the letters as you write:

ן

ן

Find and circle ב and ן in this verse:

נָבִיא מִקִּרְבְּךָ מֵאַחֶיךָ כָּמֹנִי יָקִים לְךָ יְהוָה אֱלֹהֶיךָ אֵלָיו תִּשְׁמָעוּן

The LORD your God will raise up for you a prophet like me from among you, from your brothers- it is to him you shall listen-   Deuteronomy 18:15

Look again and find the word "prophet."

Write in the correct form of nun in these Hebrew words:

אָה___   ___חְשׁוֹ___   ___זִיד

dwelling/pasture   the name "Nachshon"   soup

___חָמָה   חַ___   ___וֹ___

comfort   a famous boat builder   Joshua's father

Read aloud these real Hebrew words!

זָז אָכַל אָח אָדוֹם יוֹם אֶדֶן אָמֵן

כֵּן בָּנִים בּוֹא בִּימָה אֶבֶן אֵין

בָּם וָלָד הוּא אָהַב יַיִן טוֹבִים

לֶחֶם חֵן לֵךְ בֶּגֶד בָּנָה מֵאָה יָמָה

הָיָה דָּמִים מָגֵן לֵוִי מֶלֶךְ

Draw a picture or symbol to represent each word below:

מֶלֶךְ	לֶחֶם
יִשְׂרָאֵל	נָבִיא
לֹא	טוֹב

Lesson 20: SameCH

ס sounds like **s** as in **sun**.

ס looks like a smiley face waiting to happen. Go ahead: add two eyes and a smile to a ס. "**Sah-meCH**" even sounds like the Hebrew word for "happy": "**sah-may-aCH**." So now you have a sah-may-aCH ס.

Actually in Hebrew, that would be a " ס sah-may-aCH." Adjectives follow the noun they modify, unlike in English. As in Greek, Latin, and Latin-based languages, Hebrew adjectives change a little depending on the noun they are describing. While we could call four ladies "good" or one little boy "good," in Hebrew, the ladies would be טוֹבוֹת (**toe-vote**) and the boy would be טוֹב.

Let's take a closer look at sah-may-aCH, the word that means "happy": שָׂמֵחַ . The last syllable חַ is **aCH** rather than **CHah**. Whenever חַ is the very last syllable of a word, the vowel is pronounced first and the consonant last. This peculiarity appears in a very important Bible word: רוּחַ (**roo-aCH**) meaning "spirit" or "wind."

Read these aloud:

זוּחַ נֹחַ מִיחַ הוּחַ לִיחַ דוּחַ

That is Noah's name in the star.

Practice writing ס and pronounce it as you do. Add smiley faces as desired.

ס

Find and circle ס in this verse. Look out for mem sofit ם which is distinguished by having a square, rather than round base.

בַּחֹדֶשׁ הַשְּׁלִישִׁי לְצֵאת בְּנֵי־יִשְׂרָאֵל מֵאֶרֶץ מִצְרָיִם בַּיּוֹם הַזֶּה בָּאוּ מִדְבַּר סִינָי

On the third new moon after the people of Israel had gone out of the land of Egypt, on that day they came into the wilderness of Sinai.   Exodus 19:1

The ס you found was the first letter of the word "Sinai." Check back and see how to pronounce "Sinai."

Look for ס again in the verse below:

כִּי בָא סוּס פַּרְעֹה בְּרִכְבּוֹ וּבְפָרָשָׁיו בַּיָּם וַיָּשֶׁב יְהוָה עֲלֵהֶם אֶת־מֵי הַיָּם וּבְנֵי יִשְׂרָאֵל הָלְכוּ בַיַּבָּשָׁה בְּתוֹךְ הַיָּם

For when the horses of Pharaoh with his chariots and his horsemen went into the sea, the LORD brought back the waters of the sea upon them, but the people of Israel walked on dry ground in the midst of the sea.   Exodus 15:19

Now underline "Israel." Pronounce the first three words. The last word in this verse means "the sea." Which part means "the" and which means "sea"?

Spell the sounds of these English words with Hebrew letters:

English word	spell it with Hebrew	English word	spell it with Hebrew
sail		sight	
sea		Loch Ness	
lame		my	
less		knave	
boom		hail	
mean		nose	
maybe		dean	
moody		men	
no		cell	
mow		case	
lace		set	

Match the Hebrew words and their translations:

life   חָכְמָה

grace   יֵשׁוּעַ

wisdom   מְאֹד

steadfast love   חַיִּים

honor   דָּבָר

Jesus   חֶסֶד

very   חֵן

word/thing   כָּבוֹד

Lesson 21: Ayin

עַ (**aye-yeen**) is silent, but was not always so. עַ represented the glottal stop. That may not tell you much because we do very little glottal stopping in English outside of London. עַ once signaled the reader to make a puff of breath by tightening the back of the throat. The hyphen in "uh-oh" represents a glottal stop. Yemenite Jews preserve an ancient pronunciation and keep עַ in business, but otherwise, עַ is now silent, like אָ. Pronounce only the vowel that follows עַ.

עֵץ (**etts**) means "tree." Try translating: עֵץ חַיִּים

We could translate that phrase "a tree of life." Find a tree of life in this Bible verse:

עֵץ־חַיִּים הִיא לַמַּחֲזִיקִים בָּהּ וְתֹמְכֶיהָ מְאֻשָּׁר

She is a tree of life to those who lay hold of her; those who hold her fast are called blessed. Proverbs 3:18

It is a little harder to find a tree of life in the following verse. עֵץ appears with an "and" prefix. חַיִּים has a "the" prefix. You can find it:

וַיַּצְמַח יְהוָה אֱלֹהִים מִן־הָאֲדָמָה כָּל־עֵץ נֶחְמָד לְמַרְאֶה וְטוֹב לְמַאֲכָל וְעֵץ הַחַיִּים בְּתוֹךְ הַגָּן וְעֵץ הַדַּעַת טוֹב וָרָע

And out of the ground the LORD God made to spring up every tree that is pleasant to the sight and good for food. The tree of life was in the midst of the garden, and the tree of the knowledge of good and evil.   Genesis 2:9

Look again and underline עֵץ twice more. Circle "good" and "and good."

Practice writing עַ :

Read aloud:

עֵו עַל עֵט עֶנִי עָד עַז עֵל עֹז עֵד

אִיס סוֹ סַכָה סָל סֶן סַה סֵד סוּס

טַט מֵלִי מִיס סֵט טֶם מָל מֵם מֵט

נוֹן נֶגֶב נִיז נָל בֶן נֵג נִי נַה נֵע

יוּס טֶם יֵט לִים לֵס לֵט טֶס יֶס

מֵט טַס הָס כַדוֹ מֶד נוֹךְ לֵךְ כִי

עֵט סַם טֶס לָם לֶן טִים סֵא סֵע

בֶן טֵד נֶן סוֹי הֵי חֶם טִיב עִיל

Lesson 22: Pey

פ (**pay**) sounds like **p** as in **pop**. פ (**fay**) sounds like **f** as in **fish**. A dagesh makes all the difference for pey and fey. As the last consonant of a word, פ appears as ף , fey sofit, and sounds like **f** as in **fish**.

פ begins the Hebrew word for "face," which you can read: פָּנִים . It also begins "mouth": פֶּה (**peh**). פ is even at the end of your *nose*: אַף . (As in, "Well, then, get it אַף my nose!") An eye is called עַיִן . Yes, just like the letter. To round out the features of the פָּנִים, we need the ear: אֹזֶן.

Draw a line to connect each word and feature of the פָּנִים.

עַיִן   אַף

פֶּה   אֹזֶן

פָּנִים

Write and pronounce pey, fey, and fey sofit:

Look for **פ** , **פ** , and **ף** in Proverbs 30:33:

כִּי מִיץ חָלָב יוֹצִיא חֶמְאָה וּמִיץ־אַף יוֹצִיא דָם וּמִיץ אַפַּיִם יוֹצִיא
רִיב

For pressing milk produces curds, pressing the nose produces blood, and pressing anger produces strife.

Find "nose" in the verse above. **אַפַּיִם** is "noses." Find it. Noses here means "anger" and is a wordplay on the previous line. Perhaps because noses flare and snort in anger, the nose is associated with anger in Hebrew idiom. When Psalm 106:40 says, "Then the anger of the LORD was kindled," it literally says that God's nose got hot. In Hebrew, to have a "long nose" is to be patient, but to have a "short nose" is to be bad-tempered. The Bible is full of interesting idioms, witty wordplays, meaningful names, and poetical devices that get lost in translation. As you learn Hebrew, you will be finding treasures you had missed!

Read aloud:

פָּפַע פָּן פֵּן פִּיל פֵּע פַּע פַּל פַּג פַּב פָּל פַּא

פֶּט אַף עֵיף סוּף טֶס סֵף סָא עָד

נוֹךְ פִּי פִּים הֵף כוּף פֶּנֶב עֹף עֹט

דוֹם חַף אִים דַּל פֵּן עֹט פּוֹע דַּף

Spell the sounds of these English words with Hebrew letters:

English word	spell it with Hebrew	English word	spell it with Hebrew
knife		Ed	
feet		soapy	
safe		poof	
pail		fade	

How many ways can you spell the sound "**vah**" with Hebrew letters? Write them below:

Lesson 23: Tzadi

צ (tsah-dee) sounds like **ts** as in **hats**, or **zz** as in **pizza**. צ has a final letter form: ץ tzadi sofit.

צְדָקָה (ts-dah-kah) is a vastly important Biblical word. It encompasses justice, righteousness, and salvation. Because God so many times makes clear that His idea of righteousness is not just a matter of religious ritual for His sake, but of justice for those in need, צְדָקָה came to mean charity, too. Jesus uses it this way in the Sermon on the Mount (Matthew 6:1-2a):

> Beware of practicing your *righteousness* before other people in order to be seen by them, for then you will have no reward from your father who is in heaven. Thus, when you *give to the needy*...

Practice writing and pronouncing צ and ץ:

Find and circle צ and ץ in this verse:

וְיָדַעְתָּ כִּי לֹא בְצִדְקָתְךָ יְהוָה אֱלֹהֶיךָ נֹתֵן לְךָ אֶת־הָאָרֶץ הַטּוֹבָה
הַזֹּאת לְרִשְׁתָּהּ כִּי עַם־קְשֵׁה־עֹרֶף אָתָּה

Know, therefore, that the LORD your God is not giving you this good land to possess because of
your righteousness, for you are a stubborn people.   Deuteronomy 9:6

Look again and find the word that means "no" or "not." טוֹב is

well hidden with a prefix and suffix, but see if you can spot it. Did

you find it in the last word of the first line? טוֹב מְאֹד!

Though "righteousness" appears clearly in English, צְדָקָה, too,

is obscured with a prefix and suffix: בְצִדְקָתְךָ

Find the hidden English sentences by reading these aloud:

פִּיד אוּץ טוּ מַי גוֹץ.

לֶץ אִיט פִּיצָה.

הַץ אַף טוּ יוּא!

לֶץ גּוּ טוּ אַה זוּע טוּדֶא.

Read these real Hebrew words:

עָלָה   מֵאָה   פֶּה   לֶץ   סוּף   חָמֵץ   עִם

עֵגֶל   אָסַף   אַף   כָּנָף   פַּעַם   צָפוּן   אֶלֶף

חַיִל   הַיּוֹם   בָּה   חִטָּה   אִם   חַג   יוֹם

פֶּסַח   כִּי   אוֹ   בָּהֶם   בָּכֶם   לָכֶם   פֶּסֶל

אֵצֶל   הֵנָּה   עַמּוֹן   מוֹאָב   זָג   נֶסֶךְ   עֵרֶץ

אַךְ   סַם   אֶדֶן   מַצָּה   סוּף   חָלָב   הָאָרֶץ

Lesson 24: Kuf

ק (**koof**) sounds like **k** as in **kite**.

ק begins the word "holy": קָדוֹשׁ (**kah-dohsh**). People, places, things, and time can be קָדוֹשׁ. To be קָדוֹשׁ is to be set apart as sacred. It is possible to be a person who is קָדוֹשׁ but not טוֹב. The corrupt High Priest Caiaphas was קָדוֹשׁ because he held priestly office, though he did not practice צְדָקָה.

There is no such confusion when קָדוֹשׁ applies to God. He is altogether קָדוֹשׁ and altogether טוֹב. Isaiah had a vision of the eternal Heavenly Temple and heard the seraphim say:

קָדוֹשׁ קָדוֹשׁ קָדוֹשׁ יְהוָה צְבָאוֹת מְלֹא כָל־הָאָרֶץ כְּבוֹדוֹ

See קָדוֹשׁ there three times? Repetition is an intensifier in Hebrew. That is, קָדוֹשׁ means "holy," קָדוֹשׁ קָדוֹשׁ could mean "very holy," and קָדוֹשׁ קָדוֹשׁ קָדוֹשׁ is "incomparably holy."

Genesis 14:10 provides another example. The King James Version says the Valley of Siddim was "full of slimepits." The English Standard Version says, "full of bitumen pits." Literally, in Hebrew, "the Valley of Siddim was tarry pits pits," meaning it had a *lot* of *serious* pits.

It is not only in *word* doubling that repetition intensifies. The Proverbs often repeat an idea for emphasis, as in Proverbs 20:13:

> Love not sleep, lest you come to poverty;
> Open your eyes, and you will have plenty of bread.

How about this line from Deborah and Barak's song?

> Between her feet he sank, he fell, he lay still; between her feet he sank, he fell; where he sank, there he fell-dead.

Get the picture? And Joseph explains Pharaoh's repeated dream:

> And the doubling of Pharaoh's dream means that the thing is fixed by God, and God will shortly bring it about.

Write and pronounce ק:

ק

Find and circle ק in Genesis 22:2:

וַיֹּאמֶר קַח־נָא אֶת־בִּנְךָ אֶת־יְחִידְךָ אֲשֶׁר־אָהַבְתָּ אֶת־יִצְחָק וְלֶךְ־לְךָ
אֶל־אֶרֶץ הַמֹּרִיָּה וְהַעֲלֵהוּ שָׁם לְעֹלָה עַל אַחַד הֶהָרִים אֲשֶׁר אֹמַר
אֵלֶיךָ

He said, "Take your son, your only son Isaac, whom you love, and go to the land of Moriah, and offer him there as a burnt offering on one of the mountains of which I shall tell you." Genesis 22:2

Pronounce Isaac's name and find it above: יִצְחָק

Read aloud and copy these real Hebrew words:

חָזָק   צְדָקָה   יִצְחָק   קוֹל

strong   righteousness   Isaac   a voice

Read aloud and copy these real Hebrew words:

קָהֵל	קַנָּא	קָצֶה	צָדוֹק
congregation	jealous	edge, border	Zadok

קָצִין	קֶצֶף	זָקֵן	מָקוֹם
a captain	wrath	old	a place

קָטָן	קַיִט	קָדוֹשׁ	קָוֶה
small	summer	holy	hope

Lesson 25: Vowel Points

אֹ = אוֹ = o as in **go**

לֹד = לוֹד = **load**

Read aloud:

נוֹ   גֹל   בוֹ   בֹּן   זֹט   הֹק   מוֹם   מֹם

סֹק   צֹב   אוֹט   עֹד   נוֹן   חֹד   מוֹד   בֹא

זֹט   קֹאל   לוֹ   לֹע   פֹּז   בְּדִיה   מְבֵי   דֹץ

אֻ = אוּ = **oo** as in **boo**

מֻד = מוּד = **mood**

Read aloud:

סֶ טֶל בֶק בֶן סֶם גוֹב סוֹד הֶז

גֶף פֶל פוּל פְּלָא טַךְ מֶן בִּידוּ בְּדוּ

זֶז פְלָה גֶּפֶד עֶא וְדוּ קֶל לִיסוּ בָּא

Draw a picture or symbol to represent each word below:

פָּנִים	עֵץ
פֶּה	אַף

In each blank, write the number of the Hebrew word that best completes the sentence:

ג. לֶחֶם   ב. עֵץ   א. אֶמֶת

ו. חָכְמָה   ה. מֶלֶךְ   ד. נָבִיא

ז. לֹא

Henny Penny was on her way to see the _____.

She had been standing beneath a _____ when, all of a

sudden, a bit of sky fell and hit her on the head! The

_____ was, a nut had fallen, but Henny Penny was not

what you would call "full of _____."

Meanwhile, Little Red Hen was looking for help to bake some

_____. When she asked Henny Penny as she hurried

by, Henny Penny replicd, "_____! Not I. I must give the king

an important message!"

"Oh!" exclaimed Little Red Hen, "Are you a

_____?"

Lesson 26: Resh

ר

ר (**raysh**) sounds like **r** as in **red**.

רַחֲמִים (**rah-CHah-meem**) means "tender compassion and affection." It is the plural of the word for "womb," meaning this is the kind of wonderful love a mother has for her babies. Such love comes from God, Who the Bible says is full of

רַחֲמִים for His children.

In Hebrew, the heart is not the lovey-dovey organ of the body. The heart is the seat of one's will and thoughts. The guts are the sweet, loving, sympathetic spot. You will have to be ready for this as you read the Bible in Hebrew. Otherwise, it may come as a shock to read that when Joseph sees Benjamin, his wombs warm up! See what your translation says in Genesis 43:30.

In English, our guts are a seat of bravery, our bones of intuition, and our hearts of compassion. In the Bible, kidneys jump for joy, wombs warm up, noses burn, and guts are refreshed by kindness. May you refresh someone's guts today with wombs.

Practice writing and pronouncing ר:

ר

Find and circle ר in the Bible verse below. ר is distinguished from ד by smoothly curving around the corner. ר is distinguished from ו by having a much longer top crosspiece. Unlike ך, ר ends at the baseline and curves round the corner.

ר ≠ ד ו ך

אַחַר הַדְּבָרִים הָאֵלֶּה הָיָה דְבַר־יְהוָה אֶל־אַבְרָם בַּמַּחֲזֶה לֵאמֹר אַל־
תִּירָא אַבְרָם אָנֹכִי מָגֵן לָךְ שְׂכָרְךָ הַרְבֵּה מְאֹד

After these things the word of the LORD came to Abram in a vision: "Fear not, Abram, I am your shield; your reward shall be very great."　　Genesis 15:1

Read aloud:

פָּר בְּרָה צָאַר רוֹךְ מוֹעַ רוֹד גָּר רַא

טִיר רֶן חַר רוּבוֹ רֹאט אוֹר סֶב

פֶּר רֵלִים רֶד דְּרָה גֶּר לַרוֹר קוֹר

הָרִים קָדִי רוֹי טַעַר סוּן רַץ צֹר

צֹק לוֹ בְּרָה בִּירוֹ נֶר קֶן פַּר

Circle the syllable in each line that sounds the same as the first:

זֶד וַר נַךְ וַד נָד נַר גַד נַד

עֶם צְט אִים עִיט צָם עְס עָם

הָר כַּר כּוּ כַּד כָד בַּר בַּד כַּר

ווֹן זוּן זֹן יוֹן זֹד ווֹן זוֹן

הֹח חֹךְ הַךְ הֶךְ חק הוּךְ הֹךְ

Circle the syllable in each line that sounds the same as the first:

רֶד רוּךְ דָּר רֵד דּוֹר רוֹד רוּד

מֶם מוּם מֵם טוֹם מוֹס מוֹם

Spell the sounds of these English words with Hebrew letters:

English word	spell it with Hebrew	English word	spell it with Hebrew
road		cake	
soon		car	
oats		lake	
red		coats	
ready		wreck	
pizza		door	

Lesson 27: Shin

שֵׁ (**sheen**) sounds like **sh** as in **shine**.

שֵׂ (**seen**) sounds like **s** as in **sun**, same as ס.

שָׁלוֹם might have been some of the Hebrew you knew before learning the alef-bet, along with "amen" and "hallelujah." שָׁלוֹם means "peace" and "wholeness." It is beautifully used in Hebrew, ancient and modern, as a greeting and farewell. You can substitute שָׁלוֹם for "hi" and "bye." Try it this week. Or you might like to greet your friends with שָׁלוֹם וּבְרָכָה (**shah-lome oov-rah-CHah**) : "peace and blessing." Similarly, שָׁלוֹם עֲלֵיכֶם (**shah-lome ah-lay-CHem**) is "Peace be upon you." I like to imagine Jesus showing up in that locked room and saying cheerily, "שָׁלוֹם עֲלֵיכֶם."

To ask, "How are you?" in Hebrew is to ask, "How's your peace?" שְׁלוֹמֶךָ מַה (mah sh'lohm-CHah) In שְׁלוֹמֶךָ, do you see how the consonants of שָׁלוֹם held steady even though vowels changed and a suffix was added?

Did you notice that there was not a question mark? You will not see one in the Hebrew Scriptures. No commas, semi-colons, periods, or exclamation marks, either! What looks like a colon (׃) separates verses. When you read a Hebrew Bible you might see all sorts of strange little marks that are not vowels you have met. These are marks for punctuation or liturgical singing (cantillation). Examples surround this sentence.

Write and pronounce שׂ and שׁ:

Find and circle שׁ:

וַיִּקַּח אַבְרָם אֶת־שָׂרַי אִשְׁתּוֹ וְאֶת־לוֹט בֶּן־אָחִיו וְאֶת־כָּל־רְכוּשָׁם
אֲשֶׁר רָכָשׁוּ וְאֶת־הַנֶּפֶשׁ אֲשֶׁר־עָשׂוּ בְחָרָן וַיֵּצְאוּ לָלֶכֶת אַרְצָה כְּנַעַן
וַיָּבֹאוּ אַרְצָה כְּנָעַן:

And Abram took Sarai his wife, and Lot his brother's son, and all their possessions that they had gathered, and all the people that they had acquired in Haran, and they set out to go to the land of Canaan.   Genesis 12:5

Look again and underline שׂ.

Read aloud:

שֹׁד שִׁיה שָׂא שׁוֹל שׁוּ שֵׁם שֶׁע

This is שׁ plus the vowel *X*, and then a dalet.

Keep on reading:

שׁוֹט שֶׁע שׁוֹל שַׁב שִׁיר שָׁק שׁוּא

Read real Hebrew words:

חֹדֶשׁ שָׂרָה רַע נָשָׂא שָׁבָץ שָׁלוֹם

שָׂרִים לָקַח זָכַר סֵפֶר שׁוֹמֵר רָשָׁע

Keep on reading:

עֶשֶׂר שָׂרָה שָׂרֵי רֹאשׁ שָׁנָה שָׂנֵא

שֹׁפֵר אִישֶׁךְ אִישׁ רֶמֶשׂ אֲשֶׁר שָׁמַיִם

אֵשֶׁת יֵשֵׁב שָׁאוּל הַשָּׁם שֵׁשׁ בָּשָׂר

In the sentences below, circle the English letters that make the sound of שׂ. Write a שׂ above each circle. Then underline the English letters that sound like שׁ and write a שׁ above each one:

She sells seashells by the seashore.

Three good wishes, Three good kisses I will give to thee.

I saw a ship a-sailing, A-sailing on the sea

Spell the sounds of these English words with Hebrew letters:

English word	spell it with Hebrew	English word	spell it with Hebrew
sigh		rice	
seam		doom	
shake		sheen	
sheer		deer	
dose		shine	
share		shy	
tease		shots	
moon		movie	

Lesson 28: Tav

תּ sounds like **t** as in **tart**, same as ט.

Once upon a time, תּ represented **t** as in **tart**, and ת stood for **th** as in **thin**, but modern pronunciation eliminates the **th** sound from Hebrew and considers ת and תּ to be pronounced alike.

תּוֹרָה refers broadly to God's Word and specifically to God's revelation to Moses at Mt. Sinai. Often it means the five books of Moses: Genesis, Exodus, Leviticus, Numbers, Deuteronomy. Torah means "teachings," but is usually translated "law."

Write and pronounce ת. Notice that tav is distinguished from
ח by its toe sticking out on the left.

ת

Find ת in the verse below. ת counts, too.

הֲלוֹא אִם־תֵּיטִיב שְׂאֵת וְאִם לֹא תֵיטִיב לַפֶּתַח חַטָּאת רֹבֵץ וְאֵלֶיךָ
תְּשׁוּקָתוֹ וְאַתָּה תִּמְשָׁל־בּוֹ:

If you do well, will you not be accepted? And if you do not do well, sin is crouching at the door. Its
desire is for you, but you must rule over it.   Genesis 4:7

Look again and underline the word for "no/do not." How many
times do you see "and"?

Circle the word in each line that sounds the same as the first word:

טְשִׁי   טֶשָׂא   תֵּשְׁע   הֵשָׁע   תֵּשַׁע

סוּס   שֵׁס   שׁוּט   סוּם   שֵׁם   סוּס

Circle the word in each line that sounds the same as the first word:

שֶׂה   שַׂה   הָשׂ   שֶׂה   שׂוֹ   שַׂע   שׂה

עִיר   צִיר   אָר   עֹד   עֹר   עִיד   אִיר

חֵת   הֵת   תֵת   תֵּה   חִית   כֵּט   חֶם

Read these real Hebrew words:

רַבּוֹת   שַׁבָּת   בַּת   אַתֵּן   תָּמִיד   עַתָּה

אַחֵר   כַּף   אֶחָד   בֵּית   מַכָּה   אַתָּה   לֵב

רָעֵב   תַּחַת   עַל   תּוֹרָה   דֶּרֶךְ   אַתֶּם   נַעַר

דִּבַּת   סֹלֶת   חֵרֶם   דַּי   הֵנָּה   עוֹר   לָבָן

טָמֵא   פָּתִיל   חוֹתָם   טוּר   חֵשֶׁב   עָנָן

פֶּשַׁע   צוּר   צֶלַע   זָר   קֶרֶס   נֹכַח   קָשֶׁה

בֶּצַע   לַחַץ   גּוֹרָל   אוֹת   תֵּל   צַר   דָּגָה

Use the Hebrew clues to complete the crossword puzzle with English translations.

DOWN

1. טוֹב
2. פֶּה
3. נָבִיא
4. חֵטְא
5. קָדוֹשׁ
6. תּוֹרָה
7. עַיִן
8. זֶרַע
9. וְ־
10. בַּיִת
11. חֵן
12. יִשְׂרָאֵל
13. יֵשׁוּעַ
14. גָּדוֹל

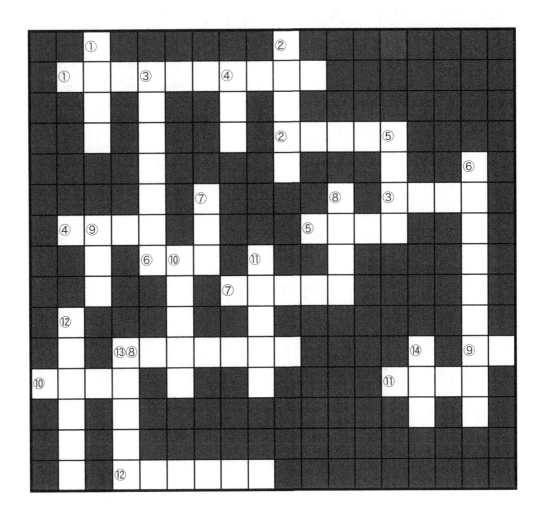

ACROSS

1. רַחֲמִים
2. אֱמֶת
3. אַהֲבָה
4. פָּנִים
5. מְאֹד
6. הַ־

7. לֶחֶם
8. צְדָקָה
9. לֹא
10. עֵץ
11. מֶלֶךְ
12. רוּחַ

Lesson 29: Sheva

Sheva שְׁוָא is a very important vowel, but it doesn't have much to say. At most, sheva provides a brief sound like the **a** as in **ago**. At the end of many syllables, sheva is silent and the consonant simply closes out the syllable. When you see sheva beneath a letter, briefly pronounce the consonant.

כ	=	כְּ
Bach	=	בָּךְ
bon-bon	=	בְּנְבֶּן
motley	=	מָטְלִי
devoid	=	דְּבוֹיד
de Gaulle	=	דְּגֶל

It would be hard to pronounce some letters with a sheva. אָ or הַ,
for example. With these letters, sheva is accompanied by another
vowel which is pronounced briefly.

בֶּ = בֶּ   דֶ = דְ

When sheva appears with the vowel אָ, they say "**oh**" together.

לוֹ = לֳ

Read aloud:

וֶ   תֳ   בֵּ   רֶד   בֶּ   מֵ   לְ   הַ   גֱ   עֲ   הֶ

Read these real Hebrew words:

קְרָב   אֲשֶׁר   אֲדוֹן   אֲנִי   מְאֹד   גְּנֹב

In Hebrew, unlike English, it is easy to read great, long words and
have no idea what you are talking about. Start at the beginning of a
word and end your syllable when you hit a sheva or the next
consonant + vowel syllable. The word's final syllable may be
"open": consonant + vowel (CV), or it may be "closed":
consonant + vowel + consonant (CVC). For example:

עָלֶ|יךָ   פָּ|נִים   מִנְ|חָה   שָׁ|מֹר   וּקְ|שַׁרְ|תָּם

CV|CV|CV   CVC|CV   stop at sheva   stop at sheva   stop at shevas

Two shevas together in the middle of a word are fun to pronounce. The first is silent. The consonant simply closes out the syllable. The second sheva will sound like **a** as in **ago**.

תִּשְׁמְרוּ

Here are some words divided into syllables. Read each syllable and then the whole word:

מְזוֹנוֹת = מְ + זוֹ + נוֹת

וְכוֹכָבִים = וְ + כוֹ + כָ + בִים

וּבִשְׁעָרֶיךָ = וּ + בִשְׁ + עָ + רֶי + ךָ

הִתְפַּלַּלְתֶּם = הִתְ + פַּ + לַּלְ + תֶּם

מַמְלְכוֹת = מַמְ + לְ + כוֹת

יִשְׂמְחוּ = יִשְׂ + מְ + חוּ

יִכְתְּבוּ = יִכְ + תְּ + בוּ

אֶצְבְּעֹתָיו = אֶצְ + בְּ + עֹ + תָיו

Divide these words into syllables and then read aloud:

יִשְׂרָאֵל   מִשְׁפָּחוֹת

מַהֲנוֹת   הֲקִימוֹתִי

וְאָהַבְתָּ   מִזְבְּחוֹתֵינוּ

בְּצִדְקָתֶךָ   לְפָנֶיךָ

נִשְׁמַעַתְּ   נִכְרַתְנוּ

הַדְּבָרִים   בְּשִׁבְתְּךָ

וְהִשְׁלַכְתּוֹ   נְבוּזַרְאֲדָן

נִשְׁתַּחֲוֶה   כְּחָכְמָתֶךָ

עֲלִילוֹתָם   לִגְבֻלֹתֶיהָ

Lesson 30: Alef-Bet

Here are the Hebrew names of the Hebrew letters in alphabetical order. Read each one aloud and write the letters next to their names. Then read and translate a word that begins with that letter.

אַהֲבָה	_____	אָלֶף	_____
בַּיִת	_____	בֵּית	_____
גָּדוֹל	_____	גִּמֶל	_____
דָּבָר	_____	דָּלֶת	_____
הַ-	_____	הֵא	_____
וְ-	_____	וָו	_____
זֶרַע	_____	זַיִן	_____

_____	חֶסֶד	_____	חֵית
_____	טוֹב	_____	טֵית
_____	יִשְׂרָאֵל	_____	יוּד
_____	כָּבוֹד	_____	כַּף
_____	לֹא	_____	לָמֶד
_____	מֶלֶךְ	_____	מֵם
_____	נָבִיא	_____	נוּן
		_____	סָמֶךְ
_____	עֵץ	_____	עַיִן
_____	פָּנִים	_____	פֵּא
_____	צְדָקָה	_____	צָדִי
_____	קָדוֹשׁ	_____	קוּף
_____	רַחֲמִים	_____	רֵישׁ
_____	שָׁלוֹם	_____	שִׁין
_____	תּוֹרָה	_____	תָּו

Lesson 31: Biblical Names

Now that you can pronounce any Biblical Hebrew that comes your way, let's meet some folks you already know, but this time in Hebrew. Can you guess the English version of these well-known Biblical names?

אַבְרָהָם _____

אָדָם _____

בִּנְיָמִין _____

חַנָּה _____

לֵאָה _____

מִרְיָם _____

הֶבֶל _____

יוֹנָתָן _____

דָּוִד _____

שִׁמְשׁוֹן _____

רִבְקָה _____

קַיִן _____

חַוָּה _____

יַעֲקֹב _____

מֹשֶׁה _____

אֵלִיָּהוּ _____

נְחֶמְיָה _____

יִרְמְיָהוּ _____

שְׁמוּאֵל _____

שָׁאוּל _____

Lesson 32: Biblical Places

See if you can match these Biblical place names to their English versions. In Hebrew, mark them on the Middle East map.

Assyria	כְּנַעַן
Babylon	פָּרַס
Egypt	עֲרָב
Persia	הַיָּם הַגָּדוֹל
Arabia	בָּבֶל
Mediterranean Sea	מִצְרַיִם
Canaan	אַשּׁוּר

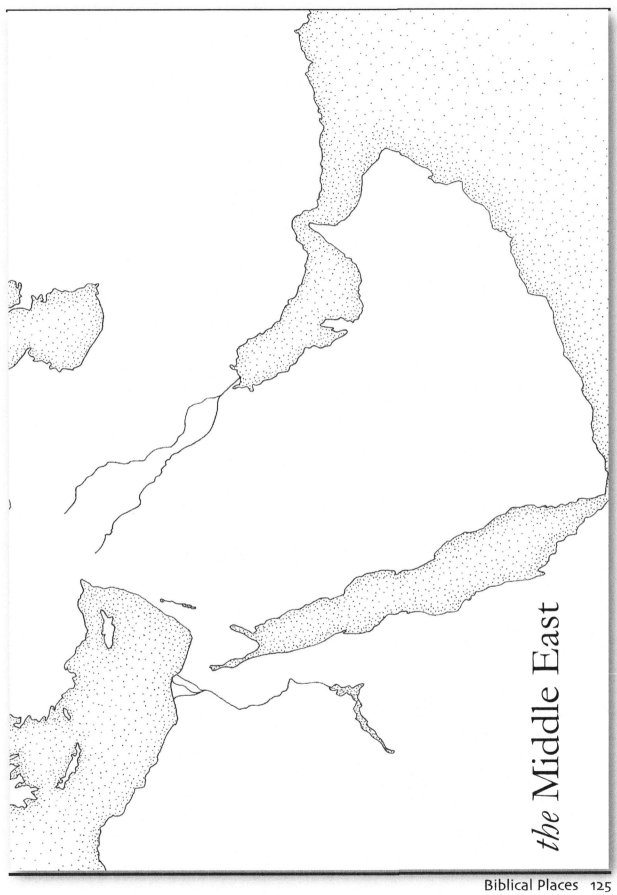

the Middle East

On the Middle East map, you marked the Mediterranean Sea: הַיָּם הַגָּדוֹל . The יָם part means "sea." Knowing that, can you translate the whole phrase? It is, literally, "the sea the big" which would translate as "the great sea," and you will find the Mediterranean called that in English Bibles.

Let's look at more Biblical place names. You will meet יָם twice again here. Match the names with their translations, then mark the places, in Hebrew, on the Land of Israel map.

Dead Sea	יְרוּשָׁלַיִם
Joppa	יָם כִּנֶּרֶת
Judah	יַרְדֵּן
Sea of Galilee	בֵּית לֶחֶם
Bethlehem	יִשְׂרָאֵל
Jerusalem	יָפוֹ
Jordan River	יָם הַמֶּלַח
Israel	יְהוּדָה

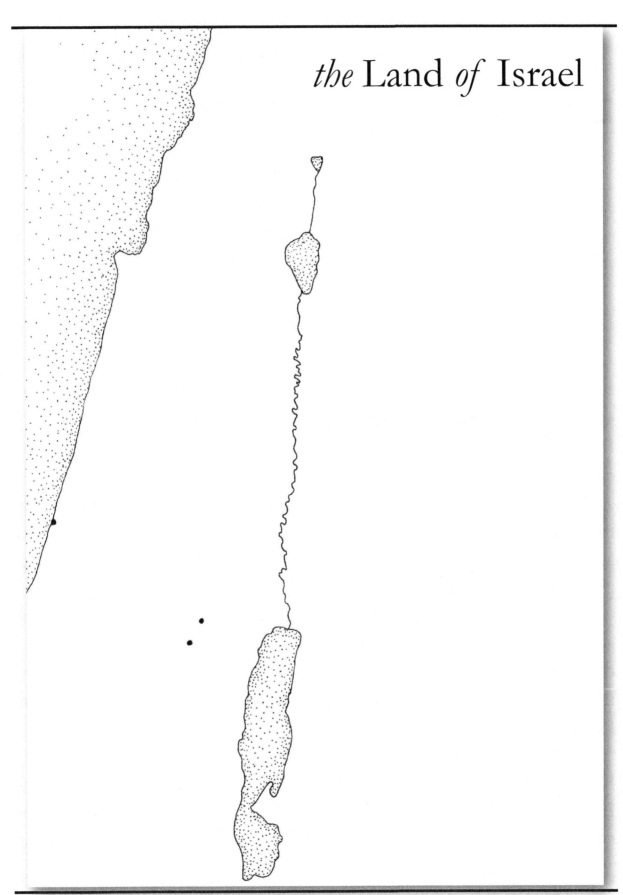

the Land *of* Israel

Lesson 33: Hebrew Bible

Let's start learning your way around the Hebrew Bible. There are already many ways you can use the Hebrew you know with a Hebrew Bible to advance your learning and to worship God! You can look up verses to find the pronunciation of names and places. *A Reader's Hebrew Bible*[1] makes this easy by showing proper nouns in gray, rather than black, letters. (No more fear when you are asked to read aloud Genesis 10 for church next week.) You can practice fluent reading straight from Scripture, even if you don't yet know what the words mean. You can look up favorite verses and memorize them in Hebrew or write them beautifully for display. You could call the books of the Bible by their Hebrew names in family Bible study, or prepare a Scripture reading in Hebrew for church.

However, there are a couple of things to get used to with a Hebrew Bible. One is that the binding will be on the *right* of the front cover. The book will seem to start on the last page. The other is that the order of books will be different from an English

---

[1] Brown II, A. Philip, and Bryan W. Smith *A Reader's Hebrew Bible.* Grand Rapids, MI: Zondervan, 2008.

translation. The Bible was written over thousands of years, and God never gave page numbers. The books will be arranged in three groups: Torah, Prophets, and Writings. The arrangement may vary slightly within these groups. Sometimes books in two volumes (e.g. 1 Kings and 2 Kings) are conflated. The following list will follow *A Reader's Hebrew Bible*, in which they are listed individually. Notice how the numbered books specify "first" and "second."

Read the names of the books of the Tanach, תַּנַ"ךְ the Hebrew Bible, aloud[1]:

Torah

Each of these books is named for its first distinctive word. The English names are not translations.

"In the Beginning" Genesis	בְּרֵאשִׁית
"Names" Exodus	שְׁמוֹת
"And He Called" Leviticus	וַיִּקְרָא
"In the Desert" Numbers	בְּמִדְבַּר
"Words" Deuteronomy	דְּבָרִים

---

[1] Tanach is the acronym for Torah תּוֹרָה, Prophets נְבִיאִים, and Writings כְּתוּבִים. " indicates a Hebrew acronym or abbreviation.

Prophets

Joshua	יְהוֹשֻׁעַ
Judges	שֹׁפְטִים
1 Samuel	שְׁמוּאֵל א
2 Samuel	שְׁמוּאֵל ב
1 Kings	מְלָכִים א
2 Kings	מְלָכִים ב
Isaiah	יְשַׁעְיָהוּ
Jeremiah	יִרְמְיָהוּ
Ezekiel	יְחֶזְקֵאל
Hosea	הוֹשֵׁעַ
Joel	יוֹאֵל
Amos	עָמוֹס

Obadiah	עוֹבַדְיָה
Jonah	יוֹנָה
Micah	מִיכָה
Nahum	נַחוּם
Habakkuk	חֲבַקּוּק
Zephaniah	צְפַנְיָה
Haggai	חַגַּי
Zechariah	זְכַרְיָה
Malachi	מַלְאָכִי

Writings

Psalms	תְּהִלִּים
Job	אִיּוֹב

Proverbs	מִשְׁלֵי
Ruth	רוּת
Song of Songs	שִׁיר הַשִּׁירִים
"Preacher" Ecclesiastes	קֹהֶלֶת
"Alas" Lamentations	אֵיכָה
Esther	אֶסְתֵּר
Daniel	דָּנִיֵּאל
Ezra	עֶזְרָא
Nehemiah	נְחֶמְיָה
"Deeds of the Days" 1 Chronicles	דִּבְרֵי־הַיָּמִים א
"Deeds of the Days" 2 Chronicles	דִּבְרֵי־הַיָּמִים ב

Hebrew Songs Copybook

Copybook Introduction

A baby learns his mother tongue by listening, imitating, and joining in. Adults living abroad often learn quickly this way, too. The task is challenging but convivial. Both the child and the expatriate accomplish more with some guidance and study.

Hearing, imitating, and joining in with Biblical Hebrew would be an effective and fairly painless way for you to soak in vast amounts of learning. If you have missed your chance to grow up in Ancient Israel, though, Part Two is for you.

Sing these traditional Hebrew songs. Learning and remembering words is much easier when they are set to music. Repeatedly read along in Hebrew as you listen or sing. Then read the lyrics without the music until you are able to do so fluently. Copy the words. Space is provided to do so twice. As you write, pronounce the words and note their meanings. Notice everything you can about words and word order.

You will be marinating your brain in Hebrew and preparing your mind for further study. (Not to mention glorifying God.)

אליהו הנביא
Elijah the Prophet

This beautiful song expresses longing for the Messiah to come with redemption. God promised to send Elijah before "the great and awesome day of the LORD"[1]. John came in "the spirit and power of Elijah,"[2] that is, he preached repentance to prepare Israel for Jesus' first coming, but he was not Elijah.[3] Elijah has been back on earth with Jesus,[4] and it may be that Elijah himself will indeed preach again before the Second Coming.[5] Elijah is called elsewhere in Jewish literature "the herald of good news." That could be translated "gospel preacher." Elijah was/is expected to teach repentance and bring the good news of Messiah's long-awaited salvation and reign. This is exactly the gospel that John the Baptist preached: "Repent. The Kingdom of God is at hand." Or, in other words, "Quit sinning. God reigns." In one sense, John *was* Elijah, Messiah *has* come with salvation, and He is Lord. And yet, we are "waiting for our blessed hope, the appearing of the glory of our great God and Savior Jesus Christ"[6] and "waiting for new heavens and a new earth in which righteousness dwells."[7] We have a lot to look forward to, and this song expresses that hope and our thirst for צְדָקָה.

---

[1] Malachi 4:5
[2] Luke 1:17
[3] John 1:21
[4] Matthew 17
[5] Revelation 11
[6] Titus 2:13
[7] 2 Peter 3:13

Elijah is welcomed at Passover meals because Passover celebrates salvation, and Messiah's coming is the ultimate salvation. In fact, it was at a Passover meal when Jesus said, "Do this in remembrance of me." Sabbath is called a "taste of the world to come" and this song is sung at the end of every Sabbath as the common working week begins again, in hopes that the week ahead holds the day of Messiah's coming, or shall we say, return.

Elijah is a spectacular hero in the Bible, and probably since everyone was on the lookout for him, he became a beloved hero of Jewish folktales, as well. In the stories, he comes in disguise, working miracles and setting wrongs to right. Recall that bystanders of the crucifixion jumped to the conclusion that Jesus might be calling Elijah for help.

The first three lines of this song are from 1 Kings 17:1 when Elijah is introduced in Scripture. You will see words you recognize here. Look for "the prophet": הַנָּבִיא.

Notice how we got the word "Messiah." "Christ" is a Greek translation of this word, meaning "anointed." Anointed means having had olive oil poured over you. In the Bible we see kings, high priests, prophets, and the Tabernacle be anointed. Messiah is the superlative king, the Heavenly priest, the prophet "like unto Moses," and the ultimate earthly dwelling place of God.

אֵלִיָּהוּ הַנָּבִיא

אֵלִיָּהוּ הַנָּבִיא,
אֵלִיָּהוּ הַתִּשְׁבִּי,
אֵלִיָּהוּ הַגִּלְעָדִי,
בִּמְהֵרָה וְיָמֵינוּ יָבוֹא אֵלֵינוּ עִם מָשִׁיחַ בֶּן דָּוִד.

אֵלִיָּהוּ	הַנָּבִיא	אֵלִיָּהוּ	הַתִּשְׁבִּי
Elijah	the prophet,	Elijah	the Tishbite,

אֵלִיָּהוּ	הַגִּלְעָדִי	בִּמְהֵרָה	וְיָמֵינוּ
Elijah	the Gileadite,	speedily	and in our days

מָשִׁיחַ	עִם	אֵלֵינוּ	יָבוֹא
Messiah	with	to us	may he come

דָּוִד	בֵּן
David	the son of

Remember to:

▸ Sing
▸ Read along in Hebrew as you listen or sing
▸ Read the words without the music until you can do so fluently
▸ Copy and pronounce
▸ Notice!

אבינו מלכנו

Avinu Malkenu

This song is a prayer that begins in the same way as the Lord's Prayer: **אָבִינוּ**, Our Father.

You can recognize several words here. Look for "righteousness," "steadfast love," and "and."

אָבִינוּ מַלְכֵּנוּ

אָבִינוּ מַלְכֵּנוּ, חָנֵּנוּ וַעֲנֵנוּ, כִּי אֵין בָּנוּ מַעֲשִׂים, עֲשֵׂה עִמָּנוּ צְדָקָה וָחֶסֶד וְהוֹשִׁיעֵנוּ

וַעֲנֵנוּ	חָנֵּנוּ	מַלְכֵּנוּ	אָבִינוּ
and answer us	be gracious to us	Our King,	Our Father,

מַעֲשִׂים	בָּנוּ	אֵין	כִּי
deeds	in us	there are not	because

"We do not have any deeds." In other words, we do not claim merit based on our works; we are dependent on grace.

וְהֶסֶד	צְדָקָה	עִמָּנוּ	עֲשֵׂה
and steadfast love	righteousness	for us	do

וְהוֹשִׁיעֵנוּ
and save us.

Can you identify which letters form a suffix that means "us" or "our"?

שמע ישראל

Shema Yisrael

When Yeshua was asked to name the most important of God's commandments, His answer began with the words of this song from Deuteronomy דְּבָרִים 6:4: "Hear, O Israel, the LORD, our God, the LORD is one." (Mark 12: 28-34)

To say that God is One is to say that He stands alone as Creator, Sustainer, and Sovereign. Acknowledging that requires our response: "And you shall love the LORD your God with all your heart and with all your soul and with all your might." (Deuteronomy 6:5, the following verse)

Books have been written on the meaning and prayerful use of these foundational words. We will hardly exhaust the subject here, but let's get a glimpse of this song's context and the riches of its words.

Jewish prayer is lively and active. There are times to stand, bow, sing, read, kneel, rise on tiptoe, blow trumpets, whisper, strike one's chest, step forward and back. But when this verse is recited, the right hand covers the eyes to better concentrate on accepting God's reign over time, all creation, our lives and futures.

By declaring these words, we also witness to the truth that the God of Israel is the only God there is, the only hope, the only salvation, the only One to serve. When this verse is written by a scribe, the last letter of the first word and the last letter of the last word are enlarged. Together they spell "witness" and remind readers of our responsibility in representing God to the world.

The second part of this song is not from Scripture. It is a traditional response, sort of like an extra special "amen." We declare that God is One and then affirm that we are glad that is so: "Blessed be the Name of His glorious Kingdom forever and ever." Jesus no doubt prayed with these words at the Temple. They were the response of the congregation on יוֹם כִּפּוּר, the Day of Atonement, to something sublime that happened only that day. In reverence, God's sacred name was not said aloud except by the High Priest on Yom Kippur. At the sound, worshippers bowed to the ground and answered with these words.

In this verse is God's name that means "I will be Who I will be," or, in other words, "I do not change, and I keep my promises." When we sing, the real name is replaced with אֲדֹנָי "Adonai," which means "Lord." Whenever vowels are shown with the letters of the sacred name (י ה ו ה), they are only reminders to the reader to substitute "Adonai." In our English translations, the convention to respectfully represent God's name is "LORD," with all capitals but a larger first letter.

Compared with English, Hebrew is generally short on vocabulary but saturated with meaning. The trick in reading Biblical Hebrew is not necessarily to choose the one proper English equivalent, but to fathom the depth of all the meanings. This song's first word, שְׁמַע, means "hear" and also "obey." When Jesus said, "He who has ears, let him hear," he was saying, "If you have heard these words, then *act* in accordance with them."

To say these words is to declare our loyalty and to know our duty: to love God with all we've got and to love our neighbors.

שְׁמַע יִשְׂרָאֵל

שְׁמַע יִשְׂרָאֵל, אֲדֹנָי אֱלֹהֵינוּ, אֲדֹנָי אֶחָד:
בָּרוּךְ שֵׁם כְּבוֹד מַלְכוּתוֹ לְעוֹלָם וָעֶד.

אֱלֹהֵינוּ	אֲדֹנָי	יִשְׂרָאֵל	שְׁמַע
is our God, (*or*, our God)	the LORD	O Israel,	Hear

אֶחָד	אֲדֹנָי
One.	the LORD (is)

מַלְכוּתוֹ	כְּבוֹד	שֵׁם	בָּרוּךְ
of His Kingdom	of the glory	the name	Blessed (is)

וָעֶד	לְעוֹלָם
and ever	forever

מי כמכה

Who is Like You?

These words are from the Song of Moses recorded in Exodus 15:11-12, 18:

Who is like You, O LORD, among the gods?
Who is like You, majestic in holiness, awesome in
glorious deeds, doing wonders?...
The LORD will reign forever and ever.

They were sung on the shores of the Red Sea in grateful celebration of deliverance.

The Song of Moses is revisited in Revelation 15 where we see the faithful singing it on the shores of a glass sea mingled with fire.

Join in the singing now by any body of water you choose.

מִי כָמֹכָה

מִי כָמֹכָה בָּאֵלִם אֲדֹנָי,
מִי כָמֹכָה נֶאְדָּר בַּקֹּדֶשׁ, נוֹרָא תְהִלֹּת,
עֹשֵׂה פֶלֶא.
אֲדֹנָי יִמְלֹךְ לְעֹלָם וָעֶד.

אֲדֹנָי	בָּאֵלִים	כָמֹכָה	מִי
O Lord?	among the gods	like You	Who (is)

בַּקֹּדֶשׁ	נֶאְדָּר	כָמֹכָה	מִי
in holiness,	magnificent	like You,	Who (is)

פֶלֶא	עֹשֵׂה	תְהִלֹת	נוֹרָא
miracles?	doing	in praises,	awesome

אֲדֹנָי	יִמְלֹךְ	לְעֹלָם	וָעֶד
The LORD	will reign	forever	and ever!

Write the phrase that means "forever and ever":

_____

Which word resembles the title of the book of Psalms?

_____

In which word of these verses does a form of קָדוֹשׁ appear?
Hint: It has a prefix attached.

_____

הנה מה טוב

Hineh Mah Tov

In this song, the words of Psalm 133:1 are put to music: "Behold, how good and pleasant it is when brothers dwell in unity!"

Just in case you have sisters, please be aware that in Hebrew the word "brothers" also means "brothers and sisters." I'm sure your folks agree fully with this verse.

You will see your old friend טוב here. Keep an eye out.

הִנֵּה מַה טוֹב

הִנֵּה מַה טוֹב וּמַה נָּעִים
שֶׁבֶת אַחִים גַּם יָחַד

You may remember that in the book of Ruth, Naomi asks her friends to call her Mara. After tragedy has struck, she no longer believes the name Naomi is appropriate because it means "pleasant." Find the word here with the same meaning and note the similarity to נָעֳמִי, which is Naomi in Hebrew.

וּמַה	טוֹב	מַה	הִנֵּה
and how	good	how	Behold,

גַּם	אַחִים	שֶׁבֶת	נָעִים
as	brothers and sisters	dwell, sit down, remain together	lovely:

יָחַד
one

עושה שלום

Oseh Shalom

"May the One Who makes peace in His heights make peace for us and for all Israel. And now say: Amen." The words of this prayer begin in Job 25:2: "He makes peace in His high heavens" and end in Psalm 29:11: "May the LORD bless His people with peace!"

You will recognize שלום and אָמֵן.

Notice the translation of יַעֲשֶׂה can be "He will make, *or* May He make." Or maybe both. Isn't it great to express at once our hope *and* our confidence? With God's promises and plans, longings are assurances.

עוֹשֶׂה שָׁלוֹם

עוֹשֶׂה שָׁלוֹם בִּמְרוֹמָיו,
הוּא יַעֲשֶׂה שָׁלוֹם עָלֵינוּ וְעַל כָּל־יִשְׂרָאֵל,
וְאִמְרוּ: אָמֵן

הוּא	בִּמְרוֹמָיו	שָׁלוֹם	עוֹשֶׂה
He	in His heights	peace	Making, *or* The One Who makes

וְעַל	עָלֵינוּ	שָׁלוֹם	יַעֲשֶׂה
and upon	upon us	peace	He will make, *or* May He make

אָמֵן	וְאִמְרוּ	יִשְׂרָאֵל	כָּל-
Amen.	And say:	Israel.	all

וטהר לבנו

Cleanse Our Hearts

In this song, we ask for purified hearts that can work for God sincerely and faithfully.

"To serve" can mean "to worship" and is the same Hebrew word as "to work." Worshipping God includes working for Him. Joshua said, "I and my בֵּית will work for the LORD." (Joshua 24:15)[1] Deuteronomy 6:13 (which Jesus quoted to Satan) says, "Be in awe of the LORD, your God, and work for Him."

When you first learned alef, you met the word אֱמֶת and learned that it means "truth." Here you will see אֱמֶת again (with a prefix) translated as "with faithfulness." Hebrew teaches us that truth does not stand alone as philosophical propositions, but is bound up in the person of God and in relationship. The Biblical word for truth includes faithfulness. "True" means "true to God."

וְטַהֵר לִבֵּנוּ

וְטַהֵר לִבֵּנוּ לְעָבְדְּךָ בֶּאֱמֶת

---

[1] Bible verses on this page are my own translation, not the ESV.

בֶּאֱמֶת	לְעׇבְדֶּךָ	לִבֵּנוּ	וְטַהֵר
in truth/with faithfulness	to serve You	our hearts	And cleanse

Each of the words in this song is a compound word. Let's look at the parts to see how a Hebrew sentence is constructed:

root meaning "purify" טהר + and (tense changer) וְ = וְטַהֵר

suffix meaning "our" נוּ + hearts לב = לִבֵּנוּ

prefix meaning "to" ־לְ + = לְעׇבְדֶּךָ
suffix meaning "you" ךָ + root meaning "serve" עבד

truth אֱמֶת + prefix meaning "in" ־בְּ = בֶּאֱמֶת

אין כאלהינו

Ein Keiloheinu

אֵין כֵּאלֹהֵינוּ

אֵין כֵּאלֹהֵינוּ,   אֵין כַּאדוֹנֵינוּ,

אֵין כְּמַלְכֵּנוּ,   אֵין כְּמוֹשִׁיעֵנוּ.

מִי כֵאלֹהֵינוּ,   מִי כַאדוֹנֵינוּ,

מִי כְמַלְכֵּנוּ,   מִי כְמוֹשִׁיעֵנוּ.

נוֹדֶה לֵאלֹהֵינוּ,   נוֹדֶה לַאדוֹנֵינוּ,

נוֹדֶה לְמַלְכֵּנוּ,   נוֹדֶה לְמוֹשִׁיעֵנוּ.

בָּרוּךְ אֱלֹהֵינוּ,   בָּרוּךְ אֲדוֹנֵינוּ,

בָּרוּךְ מַלְכֵּנוּ,   בָּרוּךְ מוֹשִׁיעֵנוּ.

אַתָּה הוּא אֱלֹהֵינוּ,   אַתָּה הוּא אֲדוֹנֵינוּ,

אַתָּה הוּא מַלְכֵּנוּ,   אַתָּה הוּא מוֹשִׁיעֵנוּ.

כַּאדוֹנֵינוּ	אֵין	כֵּאלֹהֵינוּ	אֵין
like our Lord;	There is none	like our God;	There is none

כְּמוֹשִׁיעֵנוּ	אֵין	כְּמַלְכֵּנוּ	אֵין
like our Savior.	There is none	like our King;	There is none

כַּאדוֹנֵינוּ	מִי	כֵּאלֹהֵינוּ	מִי
like our Lord?	Who (is)	like our God?	Who (is)

כְּמוֹשִׁיעֵנוּ	מִי	כְּמַלְכֵּנוּ	מִי
like our Savior?	Who (is)	like our King?	Who (is)

לַאדוֹנֵינוּ	נוֹדֶה	לֵאלֹהֵינוּ	נוֹדֶה
to our Lord;	We will give thanks	to our God;	We will give thanks

לְמוֹשִׁיעֵנוּ	נוֹדֶה	לְמַלְכֵּנוּ	נוֹדֶה
to our Savior.	We will give thanks	to our King;	We will give thanks

אֲדוֹנֵינוּ	בָּרוּךְ	אֱלֹהֵינוּ	בָּרוּךְ
our Lord;	Blessed (is)	our God;	Blessed (is)

מוֹשִׁיעֵנוּ	בָּרוּךְ	מַלְכֵּנוּ	בָּרוּךְ
our Savior.	Blessed (is)	our King;	Blessed (is)

אַתָּה	אֱלֹהֵינוּ	הוּא	אַתָּה
You (are)	God;	He (not translatable)	You (are)

הוּא	אַתָּה	אֲדוֹנֵינוּ	הוּא
He (not translatable)	You (are)	our Lord;	He (not translatable)

מוֹשִׁיעֵנוּ	הוּא	אַתָּה	מַלְכֵּנוּ
our Savior.	He (not translatable)	You (are)	our King;

Look back and see if you can figure out:

the one-letter prefix that means "like": _____

the one-letter prefix that means "to": _____

the two-letter suffix that means "our": _____

Let's take apart one word and see how it is assembled:

←

prefix meaning "like"   כְ =   כְּמַלְכֵּנוּ

king (with new vowels)   מֶלֶךְ +

suffix meaning "our"   נוּ +

Did you notice the words for "who" and "he"? Learning Hebrew pronouns can be a little like that old "Who's on first?" routine. To see why, read the following aloud:

מִי is "who;" הוּא is "he;" and הִיא is "she."

ברכת המזון
Blessing after Meals

You might be used to "asking a blessing" before eating and be wondering about a blessing *after* meals. One is a commandment and one a tradition. Deuteronomy 8:10 says, "And you shall eat and be full, and you shall bless the LORD your God…" Directly following this verse and throughout Scripture, we are warned that prosperity is dangerous and we are given a defensive tactic: to praise God for His kindness and goodness to us. That is where this song comes in. It is sung to thank God after enjoying His provisions and to remind us of where it all came from and why.

Blessing God, that is, praising and thanking Him, when we have eaten is the commandment. A quick blessing even while we are still hungry is an ancient Jewish tradition. We often see Jesus doing it: "…taking the five loaves and the two fish, he looked up to heaven and said a blessing. Then he broke the loaves and gave them to the disciples…" (Matthew 14:19). The traditional words for such a blessing, then and now, are

בָּרוּךְ אַתָּה אֲדֹנָי אֱלֹהֵינוּ מֶלֶךְ הָעוֹלָם
הַמּוֹצִיא לֶחֶם מִן הָאָרֶץ

Blessed are You, O LORD, our God, King of the Universe, Who brings forth bread from the earth.

Seeing no reason to be skimpy with our praise, Bible scholars of old composed blessings for all manner of occasions. From observing a rainbow to hearing thunder, reuniting with an old friend to studying the Bible, from enjoying the fragrance of a fir tree to seeing a king, from getting dressed even to receiving bad news, there is a blessing in Hebrew.

Memorizing a blessing and using it in everyday life would be a great way to grow in Hebrew learning. Acknowledging God in the many and varied experiences of our daily lives is a great way to grow in faith. You can find a selection of Hebrew blessings in Appendix A.

Before you copy the words of this first part of the Blessing After Meals, look for some old friends. "Grace," "compassion," "steadfast love," "bread," "good," "king," and "big" are all here. They may seem disguised with different vowels, prefixes, and suffixes. Search them out and write beside each the form in which it appears in this prayer.

	טוֹב		חֵן
	מֶלֶךְ		רַחֲמִים
	גָּדוֹל		חֶסֶד
			לֶחֶם

The words in gray boxes on page 166 are Psalm 136:25.

בִּרְכַּת הַמָּזוֹן

בָּרוּךְ אַתָּה אֲדֹנָי אֱלֹהֵינוּ מֶלֶךְ הָעוֹלָם

הַזָּן אֶת הָעוֹלָם כֻּלּוֹ בְּטוּבוֹ

בְּחֵן בְּחֶסֶד וּבְרַחֲמִים

הוּא נֹתֵן לֶחֶם לְכָל בָּשָׂר

כִּי לְעוֹלָם חַסְדּוֹ

וּבְטוּבוֹ הַגָּדוֹל

תָּמִיד לֹא חָסַר לָנוּ וְאַל יֶחְסַר לָנוּ

מָזוֹן לְעוֹלָם וָעֶד

בַּעֲבוּר שְׁמוֹ הַגָּדוֹל

כִּי הוּא אֵל זָן וּמְפַרְנֵס לַכֹּל

וּמֵטִיב לַכֹּל

וּמֵכִין מָזוֹן לְכָל בְּרִיּוֹתָיו אֲשֶׁר בָּרָא

בָּרוּךְ אַתָּה אֲדֹנָי הַזָּן אֶת הַכֹּל

אֱלֹהֵינוּ	אֲדֹנָי	אַתָּה	בָּרוּךְ
our God,	O LORD,	You	Blessed (are)

אֶת	הַזָּן	הָעוֹלָם	מֶלֶךְ
(an untranslatable word that marks direct objects)	Who nourishes	of the universe,	King

בְּחֵן	בְּטוּבוֹ	כֻּלּוֹ	הָעוֹלָם
with grace,	in His goodness,	all of it,	the world,

נֹתֵן	הוּא	וּבְרַחֲמִים	בְּחֶסֶד
gives	He	and with compassion.	with steadfast love,

כִּי	בָּשָׂר	לְכָל	לֶחֶם
because	flesh (living beings)	to all	bread (food)

הַגָּדוֹל	וּבְטוּבוֹ	חַסְדּוֹ	לְעוֹלָם
great (adjective for goodness)	And in His goodness	(is) His steadfast love.	forever

לָנוּ	חָסֵר	לֹא	תָּמִיד
to us	lack	not	continually

"We have never lacked"

מָזוֹן	לָנוּ	יֶחְסַר	וְאַל
nourishment	for us	may lack, *or* will lack	and never

שְׁמוֹ	בַּעֲבוּר	וָעֶד	לְעוֹלָם
His name	for the sake of	and ever,	forever

הַגָּדוֹל	כִּי	הוּא	אֵל
great (adjective for name)	because	He (is)	God,

זָן	וּמְפַרְנֵס	לַכֹּל	וּמֵטִיב
He nourishes	and sustains	all	and does good

לַכֹּל	וּמֵכִין	מָזוֹן	לְכָל
for all	and prepares	nourishment	for all

בָּרוּךְ	בָּרָא	אֲשֶׁר	בְּרִיּוֹתָיו
Blessed (are)	He created.	which	of His creatures

אֶת	הַזָּן	אֲדֹנָי	אַתָּה
(an untranslatable word that marks direct objects)	Who feeds	O LORD,	You,

הַכֹּל
all.

אדון עולם

Adon Olam

This is a newish Hebrew song. It is only about one thousand years old. It has (so far) collected more than one thousand melodies.

אֲדוֹן עוֹלָם

אֲדוֹן עוֹלָם אֲשֶׁר מָלַךְ בְּטֶרֶם כָּל־יְצִיר נִבְרָא

לְעֵת נַעֲשָׂה בְחֶפְצוֹ כֹּל

אֲזַי מֶלֶךְ שְׁמוֹ נִקְרָא

וְאַחֲרֵי כִּכְלוֹת הַכֹּל לְבַדּוֹ יִמְלוֹךְ נוֹרָא

וְהוּא הָיָה וְהוּא הֹוֶה וְהוּא יִהְיֶה בְּתִפְאָרָה

וְהוּא אֶחָד וְאֵין שֵׁנִי לְהַמְשִׁיל לוֹ לְהַחְבִּירָה

בְּלִי רֵאשִׁית בְּלִי תַכְלִית

וְלוֹ הָעֹז וְהַמִּשְׂרָה

וְהוּא אֵלִי וְחַי גֹּאֲלִי וְצוּר חֶבְלִי בְּעֵת צָרָה

וְהוּא נִסִּי וּמָנוֹס לִי מְנָת כּוֹסִי בְּיוֹם אֶקְרָא

בְּיָדוֹ אַפְקִיד רוּחִי בְּעֵת אִישַׁן וְאָעִירָה

וְעִם רוּחִי גְּוִיָּתִי אֲדֹנָי לִי

וְלֹא אִירָא

מֶלֶךְ	אֲשֶׁר	עוֹלָם	אֲדוֹן
reigned	Who	of the world,	Lord

נִבְרָא	יְצִיר	כָּל	בְּטֶרֶם
was created.	form	any	before

כֹּל	בְּחֶפְצוֹ	נַעֲשָׂה	לְעֵת
everything	in His pleasure	He made	At the time

נִקְרָא	שְׁמוֹ	מֶלֶךְ	אֲזַי
was proclaimed.	His name	"King"	then

וְאַחֲרֵי	כִּכְלוֹת	הַכֹּל	לְבַדּוֹ
And after	the end of	everything,	He alone

יִמְלוֹךְ	נוֹרָא	וְהוּא	הָיָה
will reign:	the Awesome One.	And He	was,

וְהוּא	הֹוֶה	וְהוּא	יִהְיֶה
And He	is,	And He	will be

בְּתִפְאָרָה	וְהוּא	אֶחָד	וְאֵין
in splendor.	And He (is)	One,	and there is no

שֵׁנִי	לְהַמְשִׁיל	לוֹ	לְהַחְבִּירָה
second	to compare	to Him	(or) to be His colleague.

בְּלִי	רֵאשִׁית	בְּלִי	תַּכְלִית
Without	beginning,	Without	conclusion,

וְהוּא	וְהַמִּשְׂרָה	הָעֹז	וְלוֹ
And He (is)	and the government.	the strength	and His (is)

וְצוּר	גֹּאֲלִי	וְחַי	אֵלִי
and a rock/ refuge	my Redeemer,	living (an adjective for Redeemer)	my God,

וְהוּא	צָרָה	בְּעֵת	חֶבְלִי
And He (is)	of distress.	in a time	(from) my cords/pain

מְנָת	לִי	וּמָנוֹס	נֵסִּי
a portion,	for me,	and a safe haven	my banner,

בְּיָדוֹ	אֶקְרָה	בְּיוֹם	כּוֹסִי
In His hand	I call.	on the day	my allotment

אִישַׁן	בְּעֵת	רוּחִי	אַפְקִיד
I die (or sleep)	in the time (when)	my spirit	I will entrust

גְוִיָתִי	רוּחִי	וְעִם	וְאָעִירָה
my body (will be).	my spirit	and with	and I will awaken,

אִירָא	וְלֹא	לִי	אֲדֹנָי
I will fear.	And not	mine	Adonai (is)

"I have the LORD, so I will not be afraid."

You have learned to *pronounce* Hebrew. The next step is to *read* Hebrew, that is, to understand what the written words mean. *Translation* is a step beyond reading, in which the translator tries to capture the full, original meaning in the words and forms of another language. Basic definitions of the words to *Adon Olam* were given to you, but they do not represent how we would beautifully express the ideas in proper English. Give translation a try, if for no other reason than to appreciate the challenge of the task. Rewrite *Adon Olam* as English lyrics:

Afterword

When you first opened this book, perhaps the inscription on page six was "all Greek." Now it is all Hebrew. You can read it aloud, no doubt with elegance and aplomb, and you would be surprised how much of it you can decipher.

שִׂים שָׁלוֹם טוֹבָה וּבְרָכָה חַיִּים חֵן
וָחֶסֶד וְרַחֲמִים עָלֵינוּ וְעַל כָּל יִשְׂרָאֵל עַמֶּךָ

בָּרְכֵנוּ אָבִינוּ כֻּלָּנוּ כְּאֶחָד
בְּאוֹר פָּנֶיךָ כִּי בְאוֹר פָּנֶיךָ נָתַתָּ לָנוּ
אֲדֹנָי אֱלֹהֵינוּ
תּוֹרַת חַיִּים וְאַהֲבַת חֶסֶד וּצְדָקָה וּבְרָכָה
וְרַחֲמִים וְחַיִּים וְשָׁלוֹם

Besides recognizing the highlighted words, you might know from the songs אָבִינוּ, "our Father," and נוּ, the suffix that means "us" or "our." Maybe you can figure out even more.

These words are a prayer that יֵשׁוּעַ and the apostles would have prayed both at synagogue and at the Temple. The words go like this: *Place peace, goodness, and blessing, life, grace, and steadfast love, and compassion upon us and upon all Israel, Your people. Bless us, our Father, all of us as one, with the light of Your face, for by the light of Your face, you give to us, O LORD, our God, teachings of life and a love for steadfast love, righteousness, blessing, compassion, life, and peace.* And to that we say: אָמֵן.

Appendices

Appendix A: Blessings

Upon hearing exceptionally good news for oneself and others:

בָּרוּךְ אַתָּה אֲדֹנָי אֱלֹהֵינוּ מֶלֶךְ הָעוֹלָם הַטוֹב
וְהַמֵּטִיב

Blessed are You, O LORD, our God, King of the Universe, Who is good and Who does good.

Upon hearing thunder:

בָּרוּךְ אַתָּה אֲדֹנָי אֱלֹהֵינוּ מֶלֶךְ הָעוֹלָם שֶׁכֹּחוֹ
וּגְבוּרָתוֹ מָלֵא עוֹלָם

Blessed are You, O LORD, our God, King of the Universe, whose strength and power fill the whole world.

Upon smelling tree scents (e.g. pine boughs, cinnamon, apple blossoms):

בָּרוּךְ אַתָּה אֲדֹנָי אֱלֹהֵינוּ מֶלֶךְ הָעוֹלָם בּוֹרֵא
עֲצֵי בְשָׂמִים

Blessed are You, O LORD, our God, King of the Universe, Who creates fragrant trees.

Upon seeing a rainbow:

בָּרוּךְ אַתָּה אֲדֹנָי אֱלֹהֵינוּ מֶלֶךְ הָעוֹלָם זוֹכֵר
הַבְּרִית וְנֶאֱמָן בִּבְרִיתוֹ וְקַיָּם בְּמַאֲמָרוֹ

Blessed are You, O LORD, our God, King of the Universe, Who
remembers the covenant, is faithful to His covenant, and fulfills
His word.

Upon dressing in new clothes:

בָּרוּךְ אַתָּה אֲדֹנָי אֱלֹהֵינוּ מֶלֶךְ הָעוֹלָם מַלְבִּישׁ
עֲרֻמִּים

Blessed are You, O LORD, our God, King of the Universe, Who
clothes the naked.

*Upon enjoying seasonal and occasional happy events (e.g. eating strawberries
for the first time that summer, seeing a good friend again after six months,
buying a new bicycle):*

בָּרוּךְ אַתָּה אֲדֹנָי אֱלֹהֵינוּ מֶלֶךְ הָעוֹלָם
שֶׁהֶחֱיָנוּ וְקִיְּמָנוּ וְהִגִּיעָנוּ לַזְּמַן הַזֶּה

Blessed are You, O LORD, our God, King of the Universe, Who
has given us life, sustained us, and brought us to this season.

Upon setting out for a destination:

בָּרוּךְ אַתָּה אֲדֹנָי אֱלֹהֵינוּ מֶלֶךְ הָעוֹלָם הַמֵּכִין מִצְעֲדֵי גָבֶר

Blessed are You, O LORD, our God, King of the Universe, Who establishes the footsteps of man.

Upon the sight of lightning, majestic mountains, shooting stars, great rivers or deserts:

בָּרוּךְ אַתָּה אֲדֹנָי אֱלֹהֵינוּ מֶלֶךְ הָעוֹלָם עֹשֶׂה מַעֲשֵׂה בְרֵאשִׁית

Blessed are You, O LORD, our God, King of the Universe, Who does the work of creation.

Upon receiving terrible news:

בָּרוּךְ אַתָּה אֲדֹנָי אֱלֹהֵינוּ מֶלֶךְ הָעוֹלָם דַּיַּן הָאֱמֶת

Blessed are You, O LORD, our God, King of the Universe, the true judge.

Appendix B: Hebrew Letters

Hebrew Letter	Letter Name in English	Block	Script	Pronunciation Guide	Value
א	Alef	א	א	silent letter	1
ב בּ	Bet, Vet	ב בּ	ב בּ	B as in boy V as in very	2
ג	Gimel	ג	ג	G as in goat	3
ד	Dalet	ד	ד	D as in day	4
ה	Hey	ה	ה	H as in hen	5
ו	Vav	ו	ו	V as in very	6
ז	Zayin	ז	ז	Z as in zoo	7
ח	**CH**et	ח	ח	CH as in Bach	8
ט	Tet	ט	ט	T as in tart	9
י	Yud	י	י	Y as in yes	10

Hebrew Letter	Letter Name in English	Block	Script	Pronunciation Guide	Value
דכך	Kaf	דכך	קככ	K as in kite CH as in Bach	20
ל	Lamed	ל	ל	L as in land	30
םמ	Mem	םמ	Nየ	M as in mom	40
ןנ	Nun	ןנ	ן ו	N as in nut	50
ס	SameCH	ס	0	S as in sun	60
ע	Ayin	ע	ɣ	silent letter	70
ףפפ	Pey, Fey	ףפפ	ອອຣ	P as in pop F as in fish	80
ץצ	Tzadi	ץצ	3 ຢ	TS as in hats	90
ק	Kuf	ק	ק	K as in kite	100
ר	Resh	ר	ꭓ	R as in red	200
שש	Shin, Sin	שש	e˙e	SH as in shine S as in sun	300
ת	Tav	ת	ת	T as in tart	400

Appendix C: Vowel Points

Vowel Point, Shown with א	Sound	Hebrew Name
אָ	ah[1]	קָמֶץ
אֳ	oh	חֲטָף קָמֶץ
אַ	ah	פַּתַח
אֲ	ah	חֲטָף פַּתַח
אִ	ee	חִירֶק
אֵ	ay	צֵרִי
אֶ	eh	סֶגּוֹל
אֱ	eh	חֲטָף סֶגּוֹל
אוֹ	oh	חוֹלֶם
אֹ	oh	חוֹלֶם
אוּ	oo	שׁוּרֶק

Vowel Point, Shown with א	Sound	Hebrew Name
אֻ	oo	קֻבּוּץ
אְ	pronounce consonant[2]	שְׁוָא
אוֹי	oi	
אַי	aye	

ah = a as in mama   eh = e as in egg
oh = o as in go   ay = ay as in way
ee = ee as in sheep   oo = oo as in zoo

---

[1] This vowel sometimes represents "oh." Details in Teacher's Manual, page 33.
[2] Sheva is sometimes completely silent and sometimes adds a brief schwa (ə) sound: **a** as in **ago**. "Schwa" is the phonics term for that sound. Guess where they got the word "schwa."

Lexicon: Hebrew to English

Part One Vocabulary

seed	זֶ֫רַע	love	אַהֲבָה
sin	חֵטְא	ear	אֹ֫זֶן
life	חַיִּים	amen	אָמֵן
wisdom	חָכְמָה	truth	אֱמֶת
grace	חֵן	nose	אַף
steadfast love	חֶ֫סֶד	house	בַּ֫יִת
good	טוֹב	big	גָּדוֹל
Jesus	יֵשׁ֫וּעַ	word/ thing	דָּבָר
Israel	יִשְׂרָאֵל	the	הַ־
honor	כָּבוֹד	and	וְ־
face	פָּנִים	yes	כֵּן

justice/righteousness	צְדָקָה	no/not	לֹא
holy	קָדוֹשׁ	bread	לֶחֶם
spirit	רוּחַ	very	מְאֹד
compassion	רַחֲמִים	king	מֶלֶךְ
peace	שָׁלוֹם	prophet	נָבִיא
happy	שָׂמֵחַ	eye	עַיִן
teaching	תּוֹרָה	tree	עֵץ
		mouth	פֶּה

Lexicon: English to Hebrew

Part One Vocabulary

English	Hebrew	English	Hebrew
amen	אָמֵן	holy	קָדוֹשׁ
and	וְ־	honor	כָּבוֹד
big	גָּדוֹל	house	בַּיִת
bread	לֶחֶם	Israel	יִשְׂרָאֵל
compassion	רַחֲמִים	Jesus	יֵשׁוּעַ
ear	אֹזֶן	king	מֶלֶךְ
eye	עַיִן	love	אַהֲבָה
face	פָּנִים	life	חַיִּים
good	טוֹב	mouth	פֶּה
grace	חֵן	no	לֹא
happy	שָׂמֵחַ	nose	אַף

not	לֹא	the	הַ־
peace	שָׁלוֹם	thing	דָּבָר
prophet	נָבִיא	tree	עֵץ
righteousness	צְדָקָה	truth	אֱמֶת
seed	זֶרַע	very	מְאֹד
sin	חֵטְא	wisdom	חָכְמָה
spirit	רוּחַ	word	דָּבָר
steadfast love	חֶסֶד	yes	כֵּן
teaching	תּוֹרָה		

Phrases

Peace be unto you: שָׁלוֹם עֲלֵיכֶם

How are you? (to a man) מַה שְׁלוֹמְךָ׃ מַה שְׁלוֹמֵךְ (to a woman)

Peace and blessing: שָׁלוֹם וּבְרָכָה

Happy (any) Holiday: חַג שָׂמֵחַ

To order Alef Press books and music,
or recommended resources,
for on-line tools,
and news of upcoming publications,
come visit us at
WWW.ALEFPRESS.ORG

Made in the USA
Middletown, DE
18 June 2021